Crossway Bible Guide

Series Editors: Ian Coffey (NT), Stephen Gaukroger (OT)
Old Testament Editor: Stephen Dray

Also in this series

Dedicated to
the Carpenders Park Christian Group
that happy fellowship in which
my family and I have found
'the unity of the Spirit in the bond of peace'.

Ephesians: Crossway Bible Guide

Free to be One

Stephen Motyer

Crossway Books
Nottingham

ISBN 1-85684-091-3

Typeset by Saxon Graphics Ltd, Derby.
Printed in Great Britain for Crossway Books, Norton Street,
Nottingham NG7 3HR, by Cox & Wyman Ltd, Reading, Berkshire.

Contents

Crossway Bible Guides

Series Editors' Introduction

Today, many groups of people meet together to study the Bible and this appears to be a booming leisure-time activity in many parts of the world. In the United Kingdom alone, over one million people each week meet in home Bible-study groups.

This series has been designed to help such groups and, in particular, those who lead them. We are also aware of the needs of those who preach and teach to larger groups as well as the hard-pressed student, all of whom often look for a commentary that gives a concise summary and lively application of a particular passage. We have tried to keep three clear aims in our sights:

1 To explain and apply the message of the Bible in non-technical language.

2 To encourage discussion, prayer and action on what the Bible teaches.

3 To enlist authors who are in the business of teaching the Bible to others and are doing it well.

All of us engaged in the project believe that the Bible is the Word of God – given to us in order that people might discover him and his purposes for our lives. We believe that the 66 books which go to make up the Bible, although written by different people, in different places, at different times, through different circumstances, have a single unifying theme: that theme is Salvation.

All of us hope that the books in this series will help people get a grip on the message of the Bible. But most important of all, we pray that the Bible will get a grip on you as a result!

Ian Coffey
Stephen Gaukroger
Series Editors

Note to readers

In our Bible Guides we have developed special symbols to make things easier to follow. Every passage therefore has an opening section which is the passage in a nutshell.

The main section is the one that *makes sense of the passage*.

Questions
Every passage also has special questions for group and personal study after the main section. Some questions are addressed to us as individuals, some speak to us as members of our church or home group, while others concern us as members of God's people worldwide.

Digging deeper

Some passages, however, require an extra amount of explanation, and we have put these sections into two categories. The first kind gives additional background material that helps us to understand something complex. For example, if we dig deeper into the Gospels, it helps us to know who the Pharisees were, so that we can see more easily why they related to Jesus in the way they did. These technical sections are marked with a spade.

Important doctrines

The second kind of background section appears with passages which have important doctrines contained in them and which we need to study in more depth if we are to grow as Christians. Special sections that explain them to us in greater detail are marked with this symbol.

How to use this book

This book has been written on the assumption that it will be used in one of three ways:

● for individuals using it as an aid to personal study

● for groups wishing to use it as a study guide to Ephesians

● for those preparing to teach others.

The following guidelines will help you to get the most from the material.

Personal study
One of the best methods of Bible study is to read the text through carefully several times possibly using different versions or translations. Having reflected on the material it is a good discipline to write down your own thoughts before doing anything else. At this stage the introduction of other books can be useful. If you are using this book as your main study resource, then read through the relevant sections carefully, turning up the Bible references that are mentioned. The questions at the end of each chapter are specifically designed to help you to apply the passage to your own situation. You may find it helpful to write your answers to the questions in your notes.

It is a good habit to conclude with prayer, bringing before God the things you have learned. If you follow the chapters of this book as a guide for studying Ephesians you will find it divides up into thirty-four separate studies of manageable length.

Group study
There are two choices:

a. You can take the ten main sections as a weekly/fortnightly study.

b. You can opt for the thirty-four separate chapters as a weekly/fort-
   nightly study or divide Ephesians up for yourself using the appropriate number of chapters as a resource each time.

Members of the group should follow the guidelines set out above for
Personal Study. It is recommended that your own notes should contain:

a. Questions or comments on verses that you wish to discuss with the
   whole group.
b. Answers to the questions at the end of each section.

The format of your group time will depend on your leader, but it is
suggested that the answers to the questions at the end of each section
form a starting point for your discussions.

Teaching aid

If you are using this book as an aid to teaching others it may be helpful
for you to note that the material has been divided into ten sections as
follows:

Praise be!	1:3–14
Prayer Focus 1	1:15–23
X-Ray 1: Do you recognize yourself?	2:1–10
X-Ray 2: Do you recognize yourself?	2:11–22
The man with the camera	3:1–13
Prayer Focus 2	3:14–21
Being the church of Christ	4:1–16
The church of Christ in every-day life	4:17 – 5:21
Special relationships	5:22 – 6:9
Spiritual warfare	6:10–24

The sections provide a division of the material in Ephesians in a way
that breaks up the text without destroying the flow of teaching. Each
section contains chapters (never more than five per section) which deal
with the key points in the text. If the above sections are used it pro-
vides a ten week study course. The questions at the end of each chapter can easily be adapted for group use as appropriate.

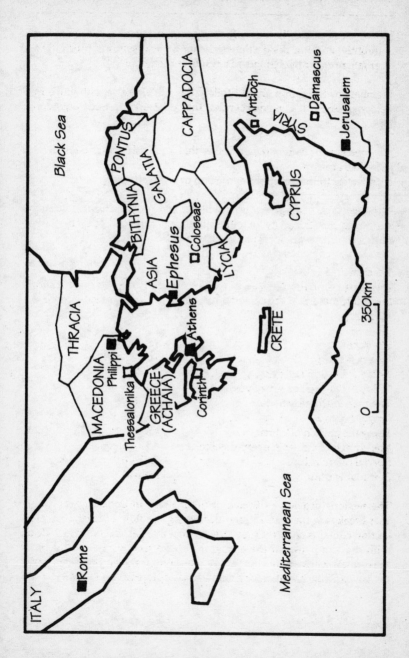

Ephesus in the time of Paul

Introduction

Ephesians 1:1–2

Paul greets the Ephesian Christians

News is important, but Paul has more important things in mind as he begins this remarkable letter.

What are the vital things to include in a letter? When I receive a letter from friends, I always feel disappointed if they don't give much news about themselves. I want to know how they are, what they have been doing, what their hopes and plans and problems are. A letter without personal news is hardly a letter at all!

So what did the Ephesians think about this letter from Paul? It contains no news about him at all, except that he is in prison (3:1; 4:1). The whole letter has been taken over by his desire to *talk to them about God*.

This seems a bit strange. In the course of the letter, Paul tells the Ephesians how much he relies on their prayers for him (6:19–20). But how can they pray for him intelligently, if he does not give them personal news about himself?

The answer to this puzzle comes at the end of the letter, in 6:21–22. 'Tychicus, the dear brother and faithful servant in the Lord, will tell you everything, so that you also may know how I am and what I am doing. I am sending him to you for this very purpose, that you may know how we are, and that he may encourage you'. Rather than write down his personal news, Paul is actually sending someone with the letter, so that the Ephesians can hear directly how he is.

This helps us to see Paul's priorities. He could have done it the other way round. He could have written down his personal news

13

and needs, and then said to Tychicus, 'Do encourage them in the Lord. Why not pass on to them what I said about Spiritual Warfare last Sunday? Oh, and remind them that Christ is the Head of the Church and they are his Body, and tell them what this means!'

But Paul doesn't do it that way, because he is 'an apostle of Christ Jesus by the will of God' (1:1), that is, *an official messenger acting on behalf of Jesus* (this is what 'apostle' means). So his absolute priority is to *talk about Jesus*, wherever he is and by whatever means he can. He actually asks the Ephesians to pray 'that whenever I open my mouth, words may be given me so that I will fearlessly make known the mystery of the gospel' (6:19). And so when he writes he wastes no time on chit-chat but gets straight down to business: 'Praise be to the God and Father of our Lord Jesus Christ ...' (1:3)!

He even changes the greeting at the start of his letter. Normally letters began like this:

Marcus (name of sender)

To his mother (name of recipient)

Greetings!

But this is not good enough for Paul the apostle of Jesus Christ. He alters the pattern:

Paul (name of sender)

To the Ephesians (name of recipient)

Grace and peace to you from God our Father and the Lord Jesus Christ!

He turns the usual vague 'Greetings' into a powerful prayer. He wants the letter to bring to the Ephesians not just his personal greetings but, far more importantly, *a new experience of the grace and peace of God in Jesus Christ*.

This is very important for us now, the readers of this letter. What do we expect to get out of reading and studying it? Just 'news', head-knowledge about Paul and his teaching? We could gain something far more important and life-changing than that. A whole new experience of the grace of God, giving us something in desperately short supply today: *Peace*, both to enjoy for ourselves and to pass on to others.

Questions
1. What kind of 'peace' do you think Paul wants his readers to experience? How can studying a book like Ephesians give us 'peace'?
2. When we write letters, do you think we should copy Paul and write all about the Lord and hardly anything about ourselves? If not, why not?

Paul and the Ephesians

Paul spent a long time ministering in Ephesus. Luke tells the story in Acts 19 and 20. Paul visited Ephesus briefly at the end of his second missionary journey (Acts 18:19–21), promising 'I will come back, if it is God's will'. And God's will it was, for Paul went straight back there at the start of his third missionary journey, and spent over two years in the city. Highlights of his ministry there included:

● His daily evangelistic discussions in Tyrannus Hall (a hall for hire in the city: Acts 19:9)

● The 'extraordinary miracles' which God did through Paul in Ephesus (Acts 19:11)

● The huge bonfire built out of books of magic spells and incantations, brought by new believers who wanted to reject their former occult arts (Acts 19:19)

● The riot which shook the whole city at the end of Paul's ministry there, as local businessmen objected to their products going up in smoke because of Paul's success! (Acts 19:23–41)

● Paul's moving farewell to the elders of the Ephesian church, in which he warns them to be on their guard and commits them 'to God and to the word of his grace which can build you up' (Acts 20:17–38).

Paul wrote this letter to them some time later, either when he was

15

imprisoned in Caesarea (Acts 23:33–35, 24:27), or in Rome (Acts 28:30). It looks as though it was written and sent at the same time as Colossians, because Tychicus was also the postman for Colossians, and exactly the same things are said about him there (compare Eph. 6:21–22 with Col. 4:7–8). In fact there are many similarities between Ephesians and Colossians.

But there are a few puzzles about Ephesians.

- If Paul knew them so well, why does he say in Eph. 1:15 that he has only 'heard about' their faith and love?

- And why does he remind them of who he is in Eph. 3:2–13, as though they did not know him: 'Surely you have heard about the administration of God's grace that was given to me for you ...'?

Experts have suggested several answers to these puzzles:

- *A different time?* Perhaps there was quite a long time-gap between Paul's ministry in Ephesus and the letter – long enough for most of the church to have changed. But this seems unlikely. The interval cannot have been more than five years.

- *A different person?* Some have suggested that Ephesians was not written by Paul at all, but later by an admiring follower of Paul, who wrote a letter in Paul's name. But this too seems unlikely. The author was clearly a spiritual giant. Could this person really have written 'each of you must put off falsehood and speak truthfully to his neighbour' (4:25), while pretending to be Paul? In any case, an admiring disciple would surely have known that Paul knew the Ephesians well.

- *A different place?* Others have suggested that Ephesians was originally sent to a different church. In fact the earliest manuscripts of Ephesians do not have 'in Ephesus' in 1:1. They simply say, 'To the saints who are also faithful in Christ Jesus'. (Of course the title, 'Ephesians', does not form part of the original letter either.) But there must have been a place-name in the greeting originally, and there is some evidence that there may have been two names there.

Alternatively, it could have been written not just to the church in Ephesus itself but to all the congregations in the area of 'greater Ephesus'. It was a very big place, one of the biggest cities in the Roman empire, with a population estimated at 250,000. Many of the suburbs and nearer towns could also have had house-churches, with members who would not necessarily have known Paul well. Perhaps the letter originally had a rather complicated address at the start, listing some of these little-known suburbs and villages. We can imagine some of the earliest scribes leaving out this list altogether when copying the letter, while others simplified it to 'in Ephesus'.

As we shall see, Paul says things in this letter which make it very relevant to the challenges faced by believers in Ephesus. And of course to us too!

PRAISE BE!
Ephesians 1:3–14

Ephesians 1:3–6

Blessed by God the Father!

Paul 'blesses' God the Father, for his 'blessing' of us in Christ.

Ephesians is full of praise and worship. One of the special things to expect from studying Ephesians is a growth in our ability to worship God and to pray.

Ephesians is like 2 Corinthians in beginning with a ringing cry of praise and adoration 'to the God and Father of our Lord Jesus Christ' (see 2 Cor. 1:3–4). Paul simply cannot keep his worship in! It just bubbles out of him. Here at the start of Ephesians, it goes on for twelve verses (1:3–14), and in Paul's original writing it continues in one long sentence of 202 words which pours straight out of his heart (the NIV translation has divided it into sentences). Paul is not really writing a letter – he's praising onto paper.

This great opening prayer sets the scene for the whole letter. Looking over Ephesians, we meet prayer in three different ways:

- *We hear Paul worshipping.* This first prayer is all worship. As we study this prayer, we must ask ourselves: do we worship God like this?

- *We hear Paul interceding.* To 'intercede' is to pray for others, and in Paul's case worship quickly leads to intercession. There are two great prayers of intercession in Ephesians, 1:15–23 and 3:14–21, both of them full of worship as well!

- *We hear Paul teaching about prayer.* He teaches by example, of course. We are meant to learn how to pray from hearing Paul pray, as in the case of Jesus himself (see Luke 11:1–4). But he also gives direct teaching about prayer, especially in 5:17–20 and 6:18–20.

As we study Ephesians, we will see how central prayer is to its whole message.

The most striking thing about this opening prayer of worship is its *theological richness*. That is, it's a prayer *focused 100 per cent on God*, starting, continuing and finishing with him. It's a prayer in which *mind and heart are united*: Paul's heart is full of praise because his mind is full of truth. There's no lack of passion, just because there's also lots of thought. So often we let these shut each other out, feeling that deep thinking can be an obstacle to deep worshipping. But Paul says 'No!' to this.

The *careful thinking* behind this prayer comes out in its structure. It's not just a passionate outburst. Paul deals with each person of the Trinity, Father, Son and Holy Spirit in turn. His praise is all directed to *God the Father*, and he praises him *for* the other two persons of the Trinity, underlining their unity:

- Praise to the Father, who chose us (verses 3–6)! Paul worships God the Father as the *author* of our salvation.

- Praise for the Son, who redeemed us (verses 7–12)! Paul unpacks the ways in which Jesus is the *architect* of our salvation.

- Praise for the Holy Spirit, who 'seals' us (verses 13–14)! Paul explains how the Spirit gives us *assurance* of our salvation.

Each of these sections in his prayer ends with the phrase, 'to the praise of his glory!' (verses 6, 12, 14). What led God to do all this, to send his Son to redeem us and his Spirit to fill us? Yes, our need of salvation prompted him – as we shall see in Ephesians 2. But more even than that, he was prompted by his own self-interest. He desires that his glory should be praised. And so, when we follow Paul's example and pray like this ourselves, our very prayer shows that God's plan of salvation has worked. His glory *is* being praised.

This is the first reason for the importance of prayer and worship in Ephesians!

There is so much to learn, just from these opening verses of the prayer:

- We learn from the whole prayer that each person of the Trinity makes a special contribution to our salvation. But this is taught also in verse 3: '... who has blessed us in the heavenly realms with every spiritual blessing in Christ'. The *Father* blesses us *with* the Spirit *in* Christ. 'Spiritual blessing' means 'the blessing that comes with the presence and power of the Spirit'. We can only receive the Spirit, because the Father wants to give him, and Jesus has made the gift possible.

● This gift is a 'blessing', that is, God *speaks goodwill* towards us. There in heaven, the place where he reigns (see Rev. 4:1–2), God has *spoken* his love toward us (the word 'bless' literally means 'speak well of'). When God speaks, things happen! He spoke once, and a whole universe sprang into being (Gen. 1:3). But even before that, 'before the creation of the world' (1:4), he had spoken a word of love towards us.

● We 'bless' him, because he has 'blessed' us! 'Praise be' in verse 3 is literally 'blessed be' – Paul uses the same word three times in one verse. We speak well of God, because he has 'spoken well' towards us. Obviously, our words don't have creative power like his. But to *speak words of praise and love toward him* matches what he has done for us!

That's another reason why worship is so tremendously important for Christians. Relationships depend on talking. A husband and wife who never talk to each other have no real marriage. It's the same with us and God the Father. We 'bless' him, responding to the way he has 'blessed' us.

● We praise him, because *he wants us to be 'holy and blameless'* (verse 4). Paul was passionate about holiness. Later in the letter he spells out what holiness means in practice. But here he reveals his heart. He is so glad that God wants him to be holy! He longs for holiness and rejoices in it – and looks forward to it as the *goal* of God's plan for him.

Questions

1. In how many different ways does Paul refer to the will or plan of God in these verses? What does this emphasis say to you?
2. Work on a definition of 'worship'. What exactly is it? Do some (constructive!) criticism of the worship in your church or fellowship, in the light of Paul's teaching and example here.

3. In the past Christians have disagreed strongly about 'election'. Why do you think Paul mentions it here? Are there disagreements about it in your church or fellowship? Explore these differences in love.

Election and Predestination

Churches have split, and whole new denominations have been formed as a result of disagreement about the doctrine of 'election'. For instance, John Wesley, the founder of the Methodist church, had a violent public disagreement over this with his former friend and fellow-evangelist George Whitfield – and as a result the wonderful 'evangelical revival' which took place under their ministry was marred with division.

Wesley, following the teaching of the Dutch theologian Jakob Arminius, refused to believe that God chooses who will be saved and who will not. He thought that this made God cruel and took away God's right to judge the world. How can God judge us for our sin, if we remain sinners only because he has decided not to save us? And isn't faith a *decision* that we make, to believe in the Lord and follow him?

Whitfield, on the other hand, following the teaching of the reformer John Calvin, thought that passages like Ephesians 1:3–6 teach election clearly: God *chooses* those who will belong to Christ and be 'adopted as his sons' through him. And so he must also choose those who will *not* belong to Christ.

The disagreement continues to the present day!

As you weigh up this debate, these are the vital things to bear in mind:

● Maybe neither Calvin nor Arminius was right. Perhaps the truth lies in the middle somewhere.

● Do you think Paul's understanding of election takes away our will or free response to God's love? He spends three chapters later on, encouraging the Ephesians to put their faith into practice. God may have *decided* that they would be 'holy and blameless' (verse 4), but this was not going to happen automatically, without their co-operation!

- Notice the connection Paul makes between election and *love*: 'In love he predestined us to be adopted ...' (verses 4–5). Election is the way in which God *loves* us in Christ.

- And notice how Jesus is called 'the One he loves' in verse 6. Election means being brought into the same kind of intimate relationship with God that Jesus, God's Son, enjoys. He is the 'natural' Son, and we are *adopted* children (verse 5), but the intimacy is the same – for we are chosen 'in' Jesus (verse 4) and 'through' him (verse 5).

- In the long run this subject is as mysterious as God himself. Paul himself realized this, at the end of three chapters in which he tried to understand God's election of the whole *nation* of Israel – Romans 9–11. At the end, all he could do was burst out in praise and adoration, just as here in Ephesians: 'Oh, the depth of the riches of the wisdom and knowledge of God! How unsearchable his judgments, and his paths beyond tracing out! ... To him be the glory forever! Amen' (Rom. 11:33–36).

Perhaps that's the most important word!

Ephesians 1:7–12

Saved by God the Son!

Paul turns into words of praise what it means to be saved, and to belong to Christ.

Paul's worship is so *full of thought*. We shall see later in Ephesians how much importance he attaches to *the use of our minds as Christians*. As we read these verses, we can sense the years of deep thinking which led him eventually to put his praise into these words.

'In him' at the beginning of verse 7 covers everything in this section – in fact, everything up to the end of verse 14. What Paul describes here applies to those who are 'in' Christ, that is, those who have 'hoped' in him (verse 12) and 'believed' (verse 13). In fact Paul uses the phrase 'in Christ' or some equivalent, like 'in him', no fewer than eleven times in this one prayer (translations may vary in the number they reproduce).

What are the greatest blessings and benefits given to those who belong to Jesus? Paul focuses on three things in this passage. Before seeing what he says, why not answer the first question in the *Questions* section below? You may be in for some surprises as you compare your answer with Paul's.

The blessing of forgiveness (verses 7–8)   This is the first thing Paul rejoices in – so perhaps it is the most important of all. Because of the 'blood' of Jesus – that is, because of his death on the cross – we have 'redemption', then described as 'the forgiveness of sins'.

'Redemption' is an Old Testament idea. God 'redeemed' his people Israel when he rescued them from Egypt and brought them into the Promised Land (see for example, Deut. 7:8, 9:26, 13:5). It suggests the thought of being freed from a cruel and powerful master, like Pharaoh king of Egypt, and this is how Paul thinks of *sin* (see Romans 3:9, 6:22). Sins are not just wrong actions. Our wrong actions are just symptoms, like the high temperature and headache that tell us, 'You've got 'flu!' Our sins are symptoms of the power of *death* over us – and with death, the power of Satan, whom we are obeying when we sin. (See Ephesians 2:1–3!) Sin grips us and holds us, and won't let us go.

But 'in Christ' we have been set free from this power, and our sins have been forgiven. By his death in our place, Jesus has soaked up the power of death so that we have been set free from its grip.

And this is all because of God's 'grace'. It would not have happened if God had not felt sorry for us and decided to save us – just as he did for Israel in Egypt. 'I have seen the misery of my people in Egypt', God told Moses. 'I am concerned about their suffering. So I have come down to rescue them from the hand of the Egyptians!' (Exod. 3:7–8). He has done exactly the same for us, 'in Christ' – except that the enemy is not human, but spiritual. God 'lavishes' his grace on us – that is, his grace is *far stronger than the chains of sin and death*.

The blessing of knowledge (verses 9–10)   The phrase 'with all wisdom and understanding' in verse 8 leads into verses 9–10. God hasn't just forgiven our sins in Jesus. He has also *explained to us how that forgiveness fits into his plan for the whole universe*.

For Paul, to *understand* what God has done is as important as to *receive* what God has done. In fact, understanding is part of receiving. Jesus commanded us to love God 'with all your heart and with all your soul and with all your mind' (Matt. 22:37 – quoting Deut. 6:5). So that we may obey the third part of this ('with all your mind'), God has 'made known to us the mystery of his will' (verse 9). We cannot love God until we understand and rejoice in what he is doing for his world!

What is his will? Paul describes it in terms of his *ultimate* will, the *goal* towards which he is leading the whole universe. It is 'to bring all things in heaven and earth together under one head, even Christ'. More literally translated, 'to sum up all things in Christ, everything in heaven and on earth in him!' (verse 10). God doesn't just plan that *we* should be 'in Christ'. He plans that *everything* should be 'summed up in Christ'.

The 'sum' or 'summary' of something is like the top metre of a pyramid. Cut it off, and you have something which is exactly the same shape as the whole pyramid, before you removed it. And without it, the whole vast pyramid is incomplete. It sums the pyramid up. In the same way, the one word 'Jesus' is to sum up the whole world and its history!

Can you get your mind around that? Paul calls it a 'mystery' (verse 9), because it goes beyond all our present experience. We don't yet see 'Jesus' summing up the world. But God says to us: this is my plan and purpose! This vision of God's plan for the world is the heart of the message of Ephesians, as we shall see.

The blessing of a future (verses 11–12)   We might feel two doubts about this. Can God's plan be thwarted, frustrated? And how can I be sure that I form part of that plan, and haven't been left out? The second question takes Paul forward into verses 13–14, but he begins to tackle it here.

The first question gets answered in verse 11: God 'works out everything in conformity with the purpose of his will'. This does not mean that everything that happens has been directly willed by God. If I murder my wife, that would be definitely *against* God's will. All sin is *against* his will in this sense. Verse 11 means that, even when dreadful things happen which he hates, God is not thrown off course. He can take these things and turn them to positive use *within* his Plan. The shedding of Jesus' 'blood' (verse 7) was a dreadful sin, but look at what he did with that! God is able to do this with 'everything'. He can 'work out' everything so that it is 'in conformity' with his Plan, and does not frustrate it or even work against it. Mind-boggling?

But can I be sure that I feature within his Plan? Yes, says Paul. God's plan to save us is part of his wider, overall Plan for the universe. 'We were also chosen' could more literally be translated, 'we have been allotted a share'. Paul uses the word which is used in the book of Numbers to describe the 'shares' in the Promised Land which were given to each tribe of Israel (e.g. Num. 26:52–56). We have a share in the Plan! – because God is *determined* that we should 'be for the praise of his glory' (verse 12).

Questions

1. What would be *your* answer to the question, 'What are the greatest blessings and benefits given to those who belong to Jesus'?
2. Can we help God's Plan along? Or do we just have to wait until it reaches fulfilment? If we can help it along, what should we be doing?
3. What do you think being 'in Christ' means practically – for each of us individually? as a church fellowship? within our town or locality? as a denomination? for the world-wide church?

Ephesians 1:13–14

Sealed by God the Holy Spirit!

Looking to the future, Paul shows us how the Holy Spirit gives us assurance that we are God's for ever!

So far, Paul has been talking about 'us'. 'We' have redemption (verse 7), he made known the mystery to 'us' (verse 9), 'we' have been chosen (verse 11). Now he suddenly becomes more personal with his readers. 'And you also ...!' (verse 13). 'We' seems to mean all Christians, the whole church. Now Paul wants the Ephesians to know for sure that what is true for the church, is true for them, personally. They are counted in!

Actually they are not just counted into God's plan for *the Church*, but his plan for *the world*. Paul looked into the future in verse 10, and foresaw a 'fulfilment' for the whole of human history and the whole of creation: it's a story told for the sake of Jesus, he's the point of it all, the goal, the destination, the peak that makes climbing the mountain worthwhile. 'And that's true for you too!' says Paul in verses 13–14: 'In Christ you too have a glorious destiny!'

'In Christ' is the vital thing. Provided they are 'in' Jesus, then they will share the glorious destiny that God plans for the whole world. How can they be sure they are 'in him'?

Paul's answer focuses on the Holy Spirit. He first mentions their faith in 'the word of truth, the gospel of your salvation' (verse 13). This was the message which said, 'Believe in the Lord Jesus, and you will be saved!' (Acts 16:31). The Ephesians had believed it, in response to Paul's preaching. But Paul did not want their assurance of 'salvation' to rest on *their faith*. That's not a sure foundation. When doubts or troubles come, this foundation collapses. How can we be sure that we have believed *properly*, or that we believed *enough* to be saved? That's just the kind of doubt that destroys assurance.

So, wonderful though faith is, we need more. And God has given it. When afflicted by doubt, we must look not to ourselves but to God, and in particular to *the gift of the Holy Spirit*, which is God's word of promise to us. Paul uses two pictures here to make this point:

● The Spirit is a *seal* (verse 13). A seal is a *mark of ownership*. As Paul explains it in verse 14, we are 'God's possession', waiting for 'redemption'. In British shops it is possible to buy something – for instance a piece of furniture – and then leave it in the shop marked 'SOLD', until it can be delivered to its new owner. Sometimes the 'SOLD' sign will have the name and address of the new owner written on it. The Holy Spirit is like that! He is God's seal of ownership, stamped securely onto us, and marking us out for delivery to our new home when the day of 'redemption' comes.

● The Spirit is a *deposit* (verse 14). This word means a 'down-payment' or a 'first instalment'. Near my home a shop selling sports equipment has a notice in the window, '10% deposit secures any item!'. You make a *part* payment, and then the item is yours, even though you haven't yet paid fully. The Holy Spirit is a part-payment, or perhaps we should say a part *gift* from God to us, a first instalment of the 'inheritance' which God is determined to give us one day. And so the Spirit 'guarantees our inheritance' (verse 14). It's absolutely sure!

This must mean that *the possession of the Holy Spirit is unmistakable*. There were some Christians in Ephesus who knew exactly what Paul meant. They had been baptized by John the Baptist and knew that they should be followers of Jesus. But when Paul met them, he knew immediately that something was missing. 'Did you receive the Holy Spirit when you believed?' he asked (Acts 19:2). Paul then explained that receiving the Spirit is the distinctive mark of Christian discipleship. He prayed for them, laid hands on them, and 'the Holy Spirit came on them, and they spoke in tongues and prophesied' (Acts 19:6).

They had absolutely no doubt that they had received the Spirit of God. It does not have to be speaking in tongues or prophesying which proves his presence in us. Paul points to many different things which do this:

- unshakeable conviction in the face of persecution (1 Thess. 1:5)

- joy in the midst of suffering (1 Thess. 1:6)

- the fruit of the Spirit in our lives (Gal. 5:22–25)

- a deep awareness of God as our *Father* (Rom. 8:15f)

- a longing for God, for heaven, for release from earthly life (Rom. 8:23; 2 Cor. 5:1–5)

- the growth of love and prayer together in our lives (Rom. 15:30)

- miracles performed through us (Rom. 15:19)

- people converted through our stumbling witness (1 Cor. 2:3–5)

- having and exercising a 'gift' or 'service' that does 'good' to our fellow-believers (1 Cor. 12:4–11)

- a deep-down conviction that Jesus is the Lord, the Son of God (1 Cor. 12:3; 1 John 4:2).

All these things are evidence of the Spirit in us. Here in Ephesians Paul adds:

- a new ability to worship God from the bottom of our hearts (5:18–20)

- learning the art of perpetual prayer (6:18).

Paul has shown the first of these in this very prayer with which his letter starts. From the bottom of his heart, he adores the God who has planned to make us his, given his Son to die for us, revealed to us his plan for the whole world, and marked us for himself by his Spirit – all so that we might be 'to the praise of his glory' (verse 14).

Questions

1. What convinces you, that you have been 'marked' by the Holy Spirit? Should we be *more* convinced by things like healing, speaking in tongues and 'words of knowledge'?

2. It's a good thing to respond to a prayer like Ephesians 1:3–14 by *praying!* Try to think (with others if possible) of different ways in which you could use this passage as the basis of a time of prayer and worship.
3. You are 'God's possession' (verse 14). What are the practical implications of this – for you, for your church?

 ### Being 'sealed' by the Spirit

What exactly is this 'seal'? Various opinions have been expressed:

● Is it baptism? Some have suggested that this is the 'seal' of the Spirit on us. Baptism was called a 'seal' by some of the early church leaders, writing just after New Testament times, and Paul calls Abraham's circumcision a 'seal' in Romans 4:11. In Colossians 2:11 he draws a parallel between baptism and circumcision. So could he be calling baptism a 'seal' here?

● Is it the laying on of hands? Some have wanted to be even more precise: the 'seal of the Spirit', they say, is the laying on of hands which accompanied baptism, because through this act the Spirit was given, as in Acts 19:6.

● Is it a special experience of filling and empowering? Others have encouraged us to *seek* sealing by the Spirit as a special, unique experience which Christians should desire.

● Or is Paul speaking simply of the possession of the Spirit, which is the universal mark of all who belong to Jesus?

This last interpretation seems to be the best. In the case of the Ephesian disciples who had been baptized by John the Baptist, the gift of the Spirit was quite distinct from their baptism. Paul links this sealing with *faith*, not with either baptism or the laying on of hands. We can probably all think of Christians who show the power of the Spirit in their lives, but no-one has ever laid hands on them to mark the gift of the Spirit to them. And if sealing by the Spirit were a special experience to be sought, it seems strange that Paul assumes that all his readers have had it – especially since he did not know them all personally. In any case, he calls the Spirit a 'seal' and a 'deposit' also in 2 Corinthians 1:22, 5:5 and Ephesians 4:30, without any indication that he is only referring to some Christians, and not to all.

So it seems best to say:

- all Christians receive the Spirit as a gift from God when they believe in Christ

- this gift is God's 'seal of ownership' on them, marking them as his

- this 'sealing' by the Spirit will be obvious in their lives in different ways, although

- we can of course 'grieve the Holy Spirit of God' (Eph. 4:30) by resisting his influence upon us and suppressing the changes he makes in us.

2

PRAYER FOCUS 1
Ephesians 1:15–23

Setting the scene

Paul continues in prayer in the second half of the chapter, 1:15–23. But his prayer now has a different focus. Three key phrases help us to see what is happening:

- 'For this reason ...' (verse 15). Because all the glorious truths wrapped up in verses 3–14 *really are true*, Paul reacts by *praying*. Is that our first reaction to the truths we believe about God and Christ?

- 'I keep asking ...' (verse 17). His prayer is focused on the Ephesians. Because these things are true (verses 3–14), he has certain requests to make for them – in fact, certain things which *above all* he longs for them to have. We will need to ask ourselves: are these the things which we long for our brothers and sisters to have, more than everything?

- 'That power is like ...' (verse 19). The prayer reaches a climax with a wonderful statement of *the power of God in Christ* and its meaning for us, his people (verses 20–23).

Like 1:3–14, this second great prayer is all one sentence in the original (this time of 169 words), just bubbling onward and upward as Paul's mind moves from the Ephesians to the Lord he wants them to know.

Ephesians 1:15–19

Prayer for understanding

Paul praises God for the Ephesians' faith and love, but longs for them to grow in *understanding* of all that God has done for them in Christ.

Ephesians is an unusual letter. Romans, 1 Corinthians, Philippians, Colossians, 1 Thessalonians and Philemon all *begin* at this point, with Paul giving thanks for his readers. But Ephesians begins with the fantastic 'Blessing' in 1:3–14. This means that the Ephesians are left in no doubt about *who to thank* for their 'faith in the Lord Jesus and love for all the saints' (verse 15) – the things over which Paul rejoices here. Do they congratulate themselves for believing and loving? 'We love, because he first loved us', says John (1 John 4:19) – and that is exactly how the Ephesians would feel, after hearing verses 4–6. In fact, Paul shows them the way. He does not praise *them* for their faith and love, he praises *God* for it. Their faith and love show that *God is at work in their lives*, and so Paul thanks *him*.

But they need more than just faith and love. In fact, something is missing here. Starting his letter to the Thessalonians, Paul thanked God for something else as well: 'We continually remember before our God and Father your work produced by *faith*, your labour prompted by *love*, and your endurance inspired by *hope* in our Lord Jesus Christ' (1 Thess. 1:3; author's italics). 'Faith, hope and love' are quite a trio for Paul, as we can see in 1 Corinthians 13:13. For him they were the three essential pillars of the Christian life. But 'hope' is missing in this thanksgiving for the Ephesians.

Well, not entirely. It does appear – in Paul's prayer for them. In verses 18–19 he lists three things which, above all else, he wants the Ephesians to grasp and understand, and the first of these is 'the *hope* to which he has called you' (verse 18). It looks as though the Ephesians had a problem with *hope*, and Paul discerns the need for spiritual growth in that area. When we look at the second half of Paul's prayer (verses 20–23), we will see one reason why they may have had this problem.

Were you puzzled by some of the things Paul writes in the opening 'Blessing'? You are not alone. It looks as though Paul was aware that readers would find his words hard to understand. For he immediately prays that God will grant understanding. He asks that God will give the Ephesians 'the Spirit of wisdom and revelation, so that you may know him ...' (verse 17). The word 'know' here means something more like 'understand'. Paul is not praying that they may 'know' God, as a child might know its parent or two colleagues might know each other at work. He is praying that they might *understand* God, as a husband and wife after years of marriage or two friends who have grown into each other's shoes. If only they could know God like that!

Such understanding comes from and through the Holy Spirit, who gives 'wisdom' and 'revelation' (verse 17). In 3:2–5 Paul is going to describe how he himself received such 'revelation'. In the opening 'Blessing' he praises God for making 'known to us the mystery of his will' (1:9). *More than anything else in their Christian lives, the Ephesians need to begin to understand this revelation for themselves.* As Paul puts it in verse 18, they need to have 'the eyes of your heart ... enlightened'.

It's like the story of Elisha and his servant in 2 Kings 6:8–23. In a tight spot, with a 'strong force' of enemy troops out to capture him and besieging his home town, Elisha prays, 'O LORD, open his eyes so that he may see'. Then we read, 'Then the LORD opened the servant's eyes, and he looked and saw the hills full of horses and chariots of fire all around Elisha' (6:17). Far greater than the threat from the Syrian army, but only visible to spiritual eyes, the armies of God were there to protect his people.

That's what Paul wants for the Ephesians!

In verses 18–19 he focuses his prayer, and their attention, on three specific things which they need to 'see'. It is worth giving a literal translation of them:

- 'The hope of his calling' (that is, the *confident expectation* which we may have because God has 'called' us to be his children (1:5))

- 'The riches of the glory of his inheritance among the saints' (that is, the *sheer wonder* of what God has in store for us in heaven)

- 'The overwhelming greatness of his power towards us who believe, according to the working of the authority of his strength' (that is, God's *unconquerable power* actively deployed for us right now).

Questions

1. In which of these three areas do you think that you most need to grow as a Christian? as a local church?

2. How do you think that we might receive the kind of 'revelation' that Paul talks about here? Does it come quickly or slowly, to each of us individually or to a group together, through our minds or through our hearts?

3. What do you learn about prayer from Paul's example here?

Ephesians 1:20–23

Prayer for power

Paul's thoughts take flight as he reflects on the power of God revealed in Jesus – and on how God's power affects us, the church of Jesus.

Verses 20–23 are an expansion of the third request that Paul makes for the Ephesians (in verse 19). It's like touching a hidden button that opens a secret door in front of you and reveals a room you never knew was there! Mention *the power of God*, and Paul takes off. Here's a modern 'paraphrase' of verses 19–23:

'I pray that you will get to understand how fantastically great God's power is, his power *at work in you!* Do you want to know how to measure God's power? You measure it by seeing it in action, and by thinking about the sheer *authority* and *strength* which he exercised when he raised Jesus from the dead. And that was no mere resuscitation, you know. He wasn't just reviving a corpse. When he raised Jesus, he seated him at his right hand in the heavenly places, where he is far above all other rulers and authorities and powers and dominions – in fact you can't mention a "power" that he's not greater than! God put *everything* under his feet, so to speak, and while we're thinking of parts of the body let's mention *heads*: God made him the "head" over everything, ruler over the whole universe. And here's the fantastic thing: he's the "head" of everything *for the church*, that's you and me. If he's the "head", then the church is his "body", completing him, yes, giving *completion* and *fulness* to the one who fills the whole universe, so great is he'.

Mind-blowing? This paraphrase does not bring out all the riches of this passage, by any means. Here are two vital points to study and think over:

1. Paul uses some important Old Testament texts here. In verse 20, he uses words drawn from Psalm 110:1. Jesus quoted this Psalm and applied it to himself in Mark 12:36, and it is a key text in the book of Hebrews (see for example, Heb. 1:13; 10:12–13). In it the Messiah is pictured as a mighty King, sitting at the right hand of God, and ruling over all his enemies. No wonder Christians applied it to Jesus!

   Similarly, in verse 22 Paul uses words drawn from Psalm 8:6. This verse is also applied to Jesus in Hebrews (for example Heb. 2:6–8). Psalm 8 is about the greatness of humankind, the summit of God's creation, and by applying it to Jesus it's as though Paul is saying, 'You think you've seen human greatness – kings, saints, philosophers? You ain't seen nothing yet!' Because Jesus is *human*, a real man, and yet also exalted to the position of the highest power in all the universe, at God's right hand, he fulfils Psalm 8 far more perfectly than any other representative of the human race.

   Paul quotes these two Psalms together also in 1 Corinthians 15:25–28, where he is writing about the same thing, Jesus' position of supreme power in the universe because of the resurrection. Jesus rules the universe *as man*, and not just as God!

2. This helps us understand verses 22–23. What does it mean to call the church 'his body, the fulness of him who fills everything in every way'? And why does Paul make this point about the church here? These are the crucial points to think about:

   a. Because Jesus died and rose again, he has *joined himself to us, his church*. He has shared our world and our *death* so completely that he is for evermore one with us, his church. By 'church' here, Paul means the world-wide church.

   b. The church is his 'fulness'. Experts continue to disagree about what exactly this means. But personally I find Mark 2:21 helpful in explaining it. There the same word 'fulness' is used, to refer to the *patch* which Jesus says should not be put on an old garment. This patch is a 'new piece' or a 'fulness' which completes the incomplete garment. Never mind that Jesus says this process will lead to disaster! That's irrelevant. The point is just that the word 'fulness' can be used to describe *something which completes the incomplete*.

With the greatest reverence, but with fantastic boldness, Paul describes the church as *that which completes* Christ. He has just pictured him as a Head – in fact, *the* Head, 'head over all things'. Heads need bodies, and this head *has* a body, the Church, *for whom* he rules over all things. It was *for our sake* that he died, rose again and came to this position of supreme power! And now we are *intimately joined* to him – so intimately, in fact, that *he cannot do without us*. We know we cannot do without him. It's true the other way round as well!

c. United to him, we too are lifted above all 'powers'. This seems to be the point that Paul really wants to make to the Ephesians. This is the secret room he wants to admit them into. If only they could understand, he prays, what it really means to be 'in' Christ: that would give them hope! (I've tried to fill out the background to Paul's prayer in *A Spell in Ephesus* and '*Principalities and Powers*' below.)

Questions

1. If you are studying in a group, work together on turning this passage into a prayer, perhaps re-writing it, painting it, dancing it, setting it to music. Use the talents available in your group. And then try to use your products for the whole church in Sunday worship, if you can!

2. What do you think Paul means by the 'rule and authority, power and dominion' to which he refers in verse 21? (See *Principalities and Powers* below)

3. If Paul is thinking about the 'world-wide' or 'universal' church here, should we commit ourselves whole-heartedly to the so-called 'ecumenical movement' which seeks to remove the barriers between 'denominations'? Do you foresee any problems with this?

A Spell in Ephesus

Why does Paul lay all this emphasis on *the power of God in Christ*? We might be tempted to wonder why he expands on the third of his three requests in verses 18–19, and not on the other two. In Ephesians 1:19–23, he uses a total of seven different words for 'power' (especially in verses 19 and 21).

The answer may well lie in the situation faced by his readers, the Christians in Ephesus. Ephesus was not only one of the biggest cities in the world at that time, it also contained one of the so-called 'Seven Wonders of the World', the mighty temple of Artemis or Diana. This was an enormous temple, covering an area larger than a football pitch, with 127 massive columns holding up a huge roof, under which literally thousands of priestesses served the goddess. One of the features of the worship of Diana was that it was deeply associated with the occult and with magic practices of many kinds. Many of the inhabitants of Ephesus practised magic, including many of the Jews who lived there. We read about this in Acts 19:13–20, where Luke first describes what happened to a group of Jewish exorcists who tried using the name of Jesus in their incantations, and then – dramatically – tells how the *Christian believers* in Ephesus eventually decided that they ought to give up magic practices, and made a huge bonfire out of all their books of spells.

People who have lived in an environment like that have no doubts about the reality of powers of evil and occult forces. They have seen magic work. They have seen people under a curse become sick and die. It was like that in Ephesus. Many of the Ephesian Christians may have feared deeply what occult powers might 'do' to them. And they were not loved by their neighbours. Paul's ministry in Ephesus eventually caused a riot, when the Ephesians as a whole decided that he was attacking the honour of their great goddess (Acts 19:23–41). And doubtless, from that point on, the church which Paul founded felt exposed and vulnerable within Ephesian society.

Recent research has revealed something fascinating about Ephesians 1:19–23 and the other places in Ephesians where Paul talks about 'power' or about 'authorities'. Examples of spells and incantations, of the sort so popular in Ephesus, have survived from that time, and one scholar, Dr Clinton Arnold, has discovered that many of the same words are used! So when Paul says

● that *God* has exerted *his* 'power' in Christ (verses 19–20),

● and that *Christ* is now supreme over all the 'powers' and over every name that can be named' (verse 21, literal translation),

he is using the words which the Ephesians themselves would have used in their magic – and referring to the very 'powers' on which the enemies of the church were calling as they tried to 'get' the Christians.

Paul's use of the expression 'every name that can be named' probably refers to the practice of *piling up names* when casting spells, because just the use of powerful 'names' was thought to give *potency* to the spell.

Jesus is supreme over all these 'names' and 'powers'! So Christians need not fear them. In fact, they may replace *fear* with *hope*, because the world around holds no final threats for them. The power that *God* exercises is 'for us' (verse 19). Those two little words say so much!

'Principalities and Powers'

This is the expression used by many to refer to the four 'authorities' listed by Paul in 1:21 – the things *over which* Jesus is now supreme. Similar lists of 'powers' appear later in Ephesians at 3:10 and 6:12, and elsewhere in Paul's writings (8:38; 1 Cor. 15:24; Col. 1:16, 2:10 and 2:15). What exactly are these 'principalities and powers'? Opinions are divided between three possibilities:

● Some see these as *spiritual powers of evil*, that is, the Devil and his armies of demons. Some even want to put them into a hierarchy or spiritual power-structure, with some more powerful than others, and a kind of 'chain of command' operating between them.

● On the other hand, some want to see them as *worldly powers*, that is, forces within human society of a political, economic, religious or ideological kind. These forces, they would say, can be just as opposed to God and to Christ as anything with horns, hoofs and a tail!

● Others again want to combine (1) and (2) and argue that there is a deep and mysterious connection between them. They point to places where Paul uses these same words to refer to worldly powers (for example, Rom. 13:1; Titus 3:1), and to places where it is unclear whether he is talking about *spiritual* or *worldly* powers and could mean *both* (for example, 1 Cor. 2:6–8; Col. 2:8–10).

Before weighing this question up, you may want to look ahead to the sections on 3:10–13 and 6:10–13 in this *Bible Guide*. Important questions to consider are:

- How does the information about the 'magical' background, given above, help us here?

- Biblical background: is it helpful to look back to Daniel's vision of the four *Beasts* (Daniel 7:3–7), who are spiritual powers but who *also* represent four great world empires (Dan. 7:17)?

- Is there any evidence, in Ephesians or elsewhere, that there are spiritual 'powers' (dark angels, demons) attached to particular places – countries, towns, even streets or houses?

- What do we have to do to fight and resist these evil powers? Does it just mean prayer, or could it also mean combating horrible features of the society around us?

My own personal convictions are these:

- These are real, spiritual forces.

- They manifest themselves not just in direct 'spiritual' ways (through oppression, temptation, occult influences), but also through political and other forces in society. There can be a clear connection between these – for instance, where the economy of a country has been ruined by financial corruption, or where official atheism or religion leads to persecution of the church.

- We stand with Paul in rejoicing that no 'power' is greater than the power of Christ!

- Our primary weapon against these 'powers' is *prayer*. But we may need to focus prayer (and obedient action) on the ways in which they have corrupted society around us – perhaps through setting up night-shelters for the homeless, or counselling and caring for drug abusers. Even through such practical ministries, founded on prayer, the 'powers' are opposed.

3

X-RAY 1: DO YOU RECOGNIZE YOURSELF?
Ephesians 2:1–10

Setting the scene

Chapter 1 ends with a tremendous climax – the stunning description of the church as the very *Body* of Christ, without which he as *Head* would be incomplete. Generally, we have become quite accustomed to thinking of the church as 'the body of Christ'. It doesn't seem a *surprising* idea to us. But it would have been surprising to the Christians to whom Paul first put it. Maybe *shocking* as well. It seems almost rude to suggest that we are that closely united to Jesus – so closely that he cannot do without us, like a head without a body.

Paul needs to say more about this. He is going to return to the idea of *the church as the Body of Christ* in 4:1–16. But much of chapters 2 and 3 relates to this theme as well, even though he only mentions the word 'body' in 2:16 and 3:6. This is because, throughout these chapters, he is teaching us in different ways about *our relationship to Jesus Christ*.

Testimonies are very helpful. Whether we give our own testimony or listen to someone else's, it is so encouraging to realize that God really does touch lives, bring people to himself, and prove his power and presence in daily experience. Ephesians 2:1–10 and 2:11–22 are *two testimonies – with a difference*. They are like spiritual X-rays. Doubtless the Christians in Ephesus could tell stories rather like ours of how they heard the Gospel and discovered that it met their need. But only the apostle Paul could write the *inside story* of their testimony as he does here – peering under the surface, looking at its bones, telling it how it really is from a spiritual perspective.

A car could give a 'testimony' about the factory assembly-line: 'First I was only a body, but then this man came along and put an engine in me and wheels on me and – look at me now!' But only the factory foreman could tell the car why it had happened, and how it was all possible.

That's what Paul does here, with these two spiritual X-rays. He explains what has *really* happened to us, underlying our experience of forgiveness and new life. Actually each X-ray comes in two parts, a 'Before' and an 'After'. In both cases a picture of our true state *before* we became Christians (2:1–3; 2:11–12) is matched by a picture of the patient *after* treatment (2:8–10; 2:19–22). In between these pictures, Paul reveals *the treatment that has made the difference* (2:4–7; 2:13–18).

The point of it all is to show *God has joined us to Jesus*. Chapter 2 begins, 'As for you ...', which would be better translated 'And you too!' Paul has just described how God exercised his mighty power in raising Jesus from the dead (1:20–23). 'And you too!' This resurrection is not just true for Jesus, but God has done exactly the same for us. In fact, he has done it to us *by* doing it to Jesus.

Ephesians 2:1–3

Dead!

Paul explains vividly what we have been saved from – the 'Before' of our Christian experience.

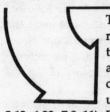 These verses make depressing reading. The X-ray reveals that things were far worse than we felt at the time. 'You were dead in your transgressions and sins!' (verse 1). 'Sin' and 'death' are closely connected throughout the Bible, because sin cuts us off from God, the source of all life (see Rom. 5:12, 6:23, 7:9–11). Perfectly 'normal' human beings, doing 'normal' things like raising families, earning a living and trying to achieve their ambitions, are nonetheless *dead* if they do not have the life which God alone can give, through faith in Jesus Christ.

These three verses begin and end with descriptions of *what we were like*:

- first, in ourselves: 'dead in ... transgressions and sins' (verse 1);

- then, as God saw us: 'we were by nature objects of wrath' (verse 3b). We may not have felt that God was angry with us. But he was.

In between these, there are three descriptions of *how we behaved*:

- *We followed the ways of the world* (verse 2a)

- *We lived in the ways of the Devil* (verse 2b)

- *We were ruled by the desires of our flesh* (verse 3a).

The world, the flesh and the Devil ... three awful enemies who had complete victory over us at that time.

What Paul writes about the Devil here would have meant much to the Ephesians. He is 'the ruler of the kingdom of the air, the spirit who is now at work in those who are disobedient'. Even before they became Christians the Ephesians would have had no doubt about the existence of hostile spiritual powers. The whole point about *magic* and indeed the worship of a goddess like Artemis, the Ephesian goddess, was to get hold of enough *power*, by one means or another, to save yourself and your family from harm (and perhaps to do harm to your enemy). And today, even in secular western societies, people are often more ready to believe in the existence of the Devil, or powers of evil, than in the existence of God.

But even when the Devil is not recognized, he is still followed. He is 'the ruler of the kingdom of the air'. This does not mean that he lives in the oxygen–nitrogen mixture that surrounds our planet. He rules over the 'atmosphere' of our world, shaping its attitudes, fuelling its conflicts, 'blinding the minds of unbelievers' (2 Cor. 4:4) – and using 'the desires of our flesh' to do this.

The NIV translates Paul's phrase 'the desires of our flesh' with the expression 'the cravings of our sinful nature'. There are impulses deep within us, as human beings, which drive us away from God and in the direction of the Devil. But these impulses are not just sinful *instincts* or *urges* that rise without warning from within us, like foul air from a sewer. We feel these 'cravings' through the 'desires' and 'thoughts' of 'the flesh' (verse 3). 'Desires' and 'thoughts' are things which go on in our minds. ('Desires' are literally 'wants' or 'will'.) Our thinking processes are all wrong. We *think* that we want the things that are best for us, but how wrong we are! Our wants are *death* to us. In fact we *are* dead – in transgressions and sins.

Questions

1. What exactly are 'the desires of our flesh'? Does Paul have sexual desires in mind here?
2. Is God angry with us whenever we sin? In what ways should the biblical teaching about 'the wrath of God' affect our Christian lives?
3. Look at the front page of a recent newspaper. Can you see signs of the power and influence of the Devil there? Can you see signs of the wrath of God? Where, in particular?

The Wrath of God

Paul sums up our 'Before' state by saying that 'we were by nature objects (literally, *children*) of wrath' (verse 3). The 'wrath' in question is that of God. His 'wrath' or 'anger' is often mentioned in the Old Testament, in fact over 150 times in all (for example: Num. 16:46; Deut. 32:22; 2 Chron. 19:10; Job 20:28; Psalm 6:1; Psalm 89:46; Isaiah 13:13; Jer. 7:20; Ezek. 7:8). A glance at these verses will show that God's 'wrath' is his *reaction against sin and evil*, and it is what leads him to *judge and punish sinners*.

Some people think that the Old Testament is full of the wrath of God, but the New Testament talks instead about the love of God. This is not true. Both Testaments speak equally about his wrath and his love. Paul's letter to the Romans refers often to God's wrath (see Rom. 1:18; 2:5, 8; 3:5; 4:15; 5:9; 9:22; 12:19; 13:4–5). But alongside this Paul writes passionately about the *love* and the *grace* of God (for example Rom. 5:5; 5:8; 8:28; 8:39; 3:24; 5:2; 5:20; 11:6).

We find exactly the same here in Ephesians. Paul talks of the *wrath* of God (verse 3) right alongside the *mercy* and *love* of God (verse 4). That is why it is vital to think clearly about what God's wrath is. His wrath is not like our human anger. Something annoys us, and we lose our temper and shout, and our anger can make us act unwisely. Then we calm down and usually begin to see things more clearly!

God is not like that. His wrath is nothing like a fit of temper. It is *the attitude which he, the Holy God, must have towards sin and those who commit sin*. But at the same time he can *love* sinners and long for them to be rescued from his own anger. It all comes together on the cross of Jesus: there we see how much God judges sin, and how much he loves sinners. Sin means death – that is, being finally rejected by the God who is the source of all life. But Jesus has borne that death for us, *sent by God to deal with the consequences of his own wrath*. How amazing!

President Calvin Coolidge of the United States of America came home from church one Sunday to be greeted by his wife. 'My dear, what was the sermon about?' Calvin Coolidge never used two words where one would do. 'Sin', he replied. 'Oh' said his wife, 'and what did the minister say about sin?' Silence while the President carefully considered his reply. And then, 'He was against it'.

It's like that with God. If God didn't object to sin, we would have no problem. But he *does* object to sin, very strongly. And so he has himself provided a way so that he can accept sinners without objection: Jesus Christ, his life, death and resurrection.

Ephesians 2:4–7

Alive!

Paul's X-ray vision reveals what God has really done for us, raising us to new life with Christ.

The famous British preacher Dr Martyn Lloyd-Jones once preached a whole series of sermons on two words: 'But God'. These two words often point to the way *God steps in* to take dramatic action in our world (see for instance Luke 12:20; Acts 2:24; Rom. 5:8; 1 Cor. 1:27). Here we have a 'But God' in Ephesians 2:4! – although the NIV has separated the two words.

God has stepped in to deliver us from our death, by *joining us to Jesus in his resurrection*. In these marvellous verses we discover three things:

1. *God's motivation.* Four things have prompted him to do this for us:

- 'His great *love* for us' (verse 4). Literally, Paul writes, 'because of the great love with which he loved us'! This points to his *willingness to sacrifice* for us.

- His *mercy* (verse 4). He is 'rich' in mercy, says Paul. This word points to his *compassion* for us, and to his longing to save us from his own wrath.

- His *grace* (verses 5, 7, 8). This word points to our lack of deserving. Nothing in us prompted him to act! It was sheer, undeserved *favour*.

- His *kindness* (verse 7). This word points to his readiness to *do for us exactly what we need*, 'in Christ Jesus'.

2. *God's action.* In a nutshell, he has done to us what he did by his power to Jesus. Compare 2:5–6 with 1:19–20. Paul uses the same words again, but adds the vital little word 'with'. When Jesus rose from the dead, he was not alone! We were there with him. We will think more about this below.

It's not *exactly* the same. Paul does not say that we have sat down 'at God's right hand', which is where Jesus has been seated (1:20). This is something special, something only for Jesus himself – the position of supreme privilege and power. But we have been 'seated with him in the heavenly realms', and therefore we *benefit* from the position and power which he now occupies.

If the Ephesian Christians were living in fear of occult and Satanic forces, we can see how encouraging they must have found this. And we can be encouraged too. Nothing can threaten those who are seated with Christ in the 'heavenly realms'! (Where exactly are these 'heavenly realms'? See *Heavenly realms – what and where* p.88)

3. *God's purpose.* Why has he done it? Verse 7 explains: 'in order that in the coming ages he might show the incomparable riches of his grace, expressed in his kindness to us in Christ Jesus'. In the long run, he has done it *for his own sake*, not for ours. He wants to 'show' his grace and kindness – like a collector 'showing' his treasures in an exhibition.

To whom does God 'show' his grace? Some Bible teachers have suggested that he wants to *prove* his love, in the face of hostile powers who dispute and challenge it. But this is probably not in Paul's mind. The book of Revelation helps us to understand. There, heaven rings with songs of praise about God's grace and love, uttered by all the inhabitants of heaven, *including* those like us who have been the *objects* of his grace and love (see for example, Rev. 7:9–12; 15:2–4). God's incomparable riches of grace are 'shown' by our very presence in heaven, as we look back and remember what he has rescued us from.

When did God 'raise us up with Christ' (verse 6)? This is quite a tricky question, to which various answers have been given.

- *At our baptism?* Some interpreters feel that Paul is thinking of baptism here, even though he does not mention it.

- *At our conversion?* Others suggest that we were raised at the moment when we first believed and were 'saved'. But many Christians cannot remember their first moment of faith.

- *At our 'sealing' by the Spirit?* Some make this a separate experience (see *Being 'sealed' by the Spirit* pp. 33–4). Could that be when we 'were raised'?

- *Somewhere around AD 30 when Jesus rose?* This suggestion seems a little strange, but it's probably right. God has already said that we were loved and chosen by him *before the creation of the world* (1:4). The fact that we were not yet born did not stop him doing that. In fact he chose us 'in Christ' at that point: he had already created a deep, deep connection between us and Jesus. So when Jesus rose from the dead, we rose with him, joined to him by the Creator God who had already set his love on us, even before we were born.

What a God! And what an X-ray. Do you recognize yourself?

Questions
1. Think of the four things which motivated God (see above). Are these things only God can show, or can we show them too? If we can, to whom should we show them?
2. What are 'the coming ages' (verse 7)?
3. At what times in our lives do we really experience what it's like to be seated with Christ in 'the heavenly realms'? Do we just have to *believe* that it is true, and *look forward* to experiencing it, or can we really experience it now?

Ephesians 2:8–10

Created!

Christians must get used to being *created*: designed, manufactured and put into service by God in Christ.

Ephesians is full of mind-boggling passages, and this one is up there with the best of them. What's so amazing about it? There are four ways in which these three verses are really very surprising:

What Paul doesn't say. What would you expect him to say next, after painting that picture of *resurrection with Christ* in verses 4–7? I would expect him to come back to the point about the 'powers' at the end of chapter one. His line of thought has run like this:

- I want you to understand how great God's power is for you (1:19).

- The greatness of his power is shown in the resurrection of Jesus (1:20).

- Jesus has been raised to a position of authority over all the 'powers' you fear (1:21–22).

- And not just Jesus! You too have been raised from the dust of spiritual death to the 'heavenly realms', because you were raised *with* Jesus (2:1–7)!

So I now expect him to say:

- So you too are exalted above the 'powers', seated there with Christ!

But he says nothing of the kind. He is so taken up with *God* that the point about the 'powers' fades from view. He goes on talking instead about the *grace of God*, about which he wants to say something even more exciting – and surprising – than anything he could say about the 'powers'.

What Paul says about grace.   In verses 8–9 he explains why God wants to show his 'grace' in the coming ages. The reason is because 'grace' is *the foundation of our salvation*. Without his 'grace', we would never have been saved. His 'grace' is close in meaning to his 'love', the love which led him to choose us before creation (1:4). 'Love' points to his *attitude* towards us, 'grace' points to his *action* towards us. Because of his love, he has *given* us his grace (see 1:6). And so he tells us very firmly that our salvation is 'not from yourselves, it is the gift of God—not by works, so that no-one can boast' (verses 8–9).

Whether they were originally Jews or Gentiles, the Ephesian Christians had all grown up with religion which told them, 'This is what you must do, if you want God to like you!' Jews had long lists of religious rules to obey, covering not just worship, but many details of every-day life. In theory they believed in the love and mercy of God, but in practice, for many ordinary Jews, this belief had got swamped by a flood of rules and regulations which made God's grace *conditional*: keep all these rules, and God will show you his favour!

It was even worse for Gentiles, especially the ones involved in magic and the occult. They would go to great lengths to say the right spells, utter the powerful 'names', perform the correct rituals, in order to get 'the gods' or a particular 'god' on their side. 'If only I can gain the favour of Artemis / Persephone / Aphrodite (the possible list is endless!), then I'll be all right!'

Against this background, what wonderful words Paul writes! They can never *gain* the favour of God by their 'works', however hard they try. But they don't have to: because God's favour is *absolutely assured*, just on the basis of *faith*. He *gives* them 'salvation' – which means total and final *safety* from all that harms, both in this life and the next.

That's what God wants to 'show'!

What Paul says about creation. Verse 10 is the climax of Paul's 'After' X-ray. But his spiritual X-ray vision spots something quite amazing about us. 'We are God's workmanship, created in Christ Jesus to do good works, which God prepared in advance for us to do'. Viewed from one angle, we have been *re*-created in Christ – lifted out of the death of sin and re-made by God with a whole new life to live, like street-kids rescued from the gutter and given a whole new start.

But viewed from another angle, Paul sees not re-creation, but simply *creation*. We existed in the mind of God even before the world was made, and at that point he set his love on us in Christ (1:4). So we were 'created in Christ Jesus'. However black our pre-Christian past may be, from God's point of view we have *always* been 'in Christ'. It just took a while for his 'call' to come through!

Some of the Ephesians looked back, I have no doubt, on some very 'black' experiences, involving dreadful evil and the horrific practices that often go with Satanic rituals. What a blessing to hear that, so far as God is concerned, that past simply does not exist. It has been dealt with by his grace in Christ. From his angle, they are 'created in Christ Jesus'.

What Paul says about works. God's plan for us covers not just our *creation*, but our *history* as well. He has planned our lives, 'prepared in advance' the 'good works' he wants us to do (verse 10). (See '*Good Works*' p.61 which looks at this more closely.) Paul actually uses the word 'walk' here (although the NIV translates it 'to do'): 'prepared in advance for us to walk in'. This 'walking' contrasts with the 'walking' in verse 2 (NIV 'to live'), where he uses the same word in talking of the 'trangressions and sins in which you used to walk'. Our whole lifestyle and direction has been turned around, and we are *taking steps* to follow God's plan for our lives. Aren't we?

Questions

1. Try to think of illustrations of 'grace'. What difficulties sometimes stand in the way of just 'receiving' from God, or from others?
2. Be honest with yourself (and with the group, if appropriate): do you carry around burdens and memories of sins past which cause you pain still? How does this passage help you?

3. Do we have to work hard to *discover* the 'good works' God has prepared for us, or will we find them automatically, without trying?

'Good works'

Paul was usually very suspicious when people talked about 'works'. He often met this talk from Jews who insisted that God had a list of 'works' for people to do, in order to gain his approval. Basically, these were the 'works' required of all Jews and converts to Judaism – circumcise your children, keep the Sabbath and the festivals, observe the food laws and the purity regulations, and be zealous for God ... and you will preserve your place in the Kingdom!

That was Paul's life before he met the risen Jesus on the road to Damascus. Then he rejected this life of 'works', because he discovered that this *zeal for God* had actually led him to hate and persecute God's Messiah and his followers! Instead, he discovered *grace*: God had stepped in to give forgiveness and a whole new life to this violent persecutor of the church. Jesus Christ had not judged Paul or rejected him because of his hatred, but loved him and given him his Holy Spirit! (Read all about it in Acts 9:1–19; Gal. 1:11–17; 2:19–21; Phil. 3:4–11; 1 Tim. 1:12–14.)

Paul argued long and hard about this whole issue of 'works'. He had to tread very carefully. On the one hand, he knew that we cannot *become* acceptable to God, or *earn* his grace, through what we do. But on the other hand, he knew that, once accepted and forgiven by him, we must love him, follow him and serve him in the power of the Spirit (see Gal. 5:2–6; Rom. 3:27–31; 7:4–6, 8:5–11). That is why he speaks of 'works' in two senses here in Ephesians:

● 'Not by works!' (verse 9): we cannot *earn* grace.

● 'To do good works!' (verse 10): we must *respond* to grace.

In what sense does God 'prepare in advance' the 'good works' in which we must 'walk'?

● Does he plan them down to the minutest detail? For instance, did he directly plan that I should spend some special time with my son last night, reading him a bed-time story?

61

- Does he write a *general* plan for our lives, including just the large things but not the details? For instance, did he just plan that my wife and I should adopt three children, but *not* the details of daily love and care?

- Or does he 'prepare' the good works in an even more general sense, just making us *the kind of people* who will be gifted for certain avenues of service? For instance, did he just plan that my wife and I would be unable to have our own children, while also giving us a deep love for children ... and then leave the rest to our decision?

Paul does not answer these questions here. He leaves us to think about them! And of course views on this differ between theologians. What do *you* think?

The vital things to bear in mind are these:

- God does not turn us into robots. He will call us to account one day for the way we have spent our lives (Rom. 14:10–12; 2 Cor. 5:9–10). Moment by moment, our lives are *our decision*.

- The old 'works' were basically the rules by which *all* Jews had to live. This might suggest that the new 'good works' are also the general 'rules' of the Christian life – prayer and worship, expressing love and service within the church, producing 'the fruit of the Spirit'.

- But it could be more than this, in that we each have a special 'calling' from God. Paul was 'called to be an apostle' (Rom. 1:1; 1 Cor. 1:1). I believe it is appropriate to talk about being 'called' in the same way into whatever job or life we have (see 1 Cor. 7:17).

- In a mysterious way, could God also plan my detailed decisions, moment by moment – provided they are decisions to do *good*, of course?

4

X-RAY 2: DO YOU RECOGNIZE YOURSELF?
Ephesians 2:11–22

Setting the scene

We have already thought about the way in which Ephesians 2:11–22 has the same *shape* as 2:1–10, contrasting 'Before' and 'After' pictures of our Christian lives, and describing the treatment which has made the difference (see above, p. 49). Paul's X-ray vision is such that, even though they serve the same purpose, the pictures in 2:11–22 are very different indeed from those in 2:1–10. Detailed differences will appear as we go along, but in general we can say this:

● 2:1–10 focuses on us *as individuals*, 2:11–22 on us *as a group*.

● 2:1–10 is concerned with *our behaviour* (both 'Before' and 'After'), 2:11–22 with *our status* before God.

● 2:1–10 addresses us as *human beings*, 2:11–22 addresses us as *Gentiles or Jews*.

● 2:1–10 is centred around the *resurrection of Christ*, 2:11–22 around the *death of Christ*.

Ephesians 2:11–13

Godless Gentiles

'Alienation' and 'reconciliation' are the long words which sum up what God has done for us in Christ. The first is replaced by the second!

We discover from 2:11 that most of the Ephesian church were Gentiles, rather than Jews. Paul talks directly to his readers: 'You who are Gentiles by birth ...'. This does not mean that there were *no* Jewish Christians there, merely that they were in a minority. In fact, what Paul says in 2:11–22 is just as relevant to Jewish Christians as to Gentiles, even though he starts off by addressing the Gentiles directly. Without doubt, most of the readers of this *Crossway Bible Guide* will be Gentiles, so that makes this section especially important for my readers, too!

Paul wants to reveal something to his Gentile readers of which they may have been completely unaware, even though he begins by telling them to 'remember' it (verse 11). Let's question a passing Ephesian Christian – Trophimus, for instance (see Acts 21:29): 'Tell us, Trophimus. You became a Christian just last year. *What was your biggest need that Jesus met for you?*' I think I can guarantee that Trophimus would *not* reply, 'I was "excluded from citizenship in Israel", and now Jesus has made me "a fellow-citizen with God's people"'! Yet that is how Paul describes it in this passage (see verses 12, 19). Would *you* say that this was your biggest need? X-ray eyes reveal so much more.

Paul wants his Gentile readers to *discover the Jewish roots of their Christian faith*. Thankfully, many Christians are doing that today, also. But it is not just a matter of passing interest. For Paul, it was absolutely vital that Gentile Christians should learn to understand *from the Old Testament* what God had done for them in Christ.

This means understanding their *need* in Old Testament terms first of all. This is what Paul tries to show them in verses 11–12. These are the main points he makes:

● The human race is divided into two, the 'uncircumcised' and the 'circumcised' (verse 11).

● Christ, that is, the *Messiah*, belongs to Israel, so as Gentiles they had no natural access to him (verse 12).

● To be a citizen of Israel was an enormous privilege, because it meant having 'the covenants of promise' (verse 12), the special promises given to Abraham and to his descendants that put them into a unique relationship with God (see for instance Gen. 17:3–8; Exod. 6:2–8; Deut. 7:7–9; 2 Sam. 7:22–26).

● But the Gentiles were 'foreigners' from Israel, excluded from the covenant, and therefore 'without hope and without God in the world' (verse 12).

Paul doesn't mention the tragedy he mourns in Romans 9:1–5 – that his fellow-Jews, even though the Messiah was *theirs*, have failed to believe in him. This is because he is simply lining up the Ephesians' experience with that of the whole world during the centuries before Christ came. Throughout that time, *Israel* was where God was, and so all who wanted to know him had to join Israel.

'But now!' These two words at the beginning of verse 13 are the whole Gospel in a nutshell. God has stepped in *for the Gentiles*, just as he once stepped in *for Israel*. The next three words are the key: 'in Christ Jesus ...'. Because of Jesus, in fact because of 'his blood', the age-long barrier between Jews and Gentiles has been broken down, and the Gentiles 'have been brought near'.

In verse 13 Paul is already reflecting the words of an Old Testament verse which he is actually going to quote more fully in verse 17. Isaiah 57 talks about how God wants to rescue all humankind, and not just Israel. '"I have seen his ways, but I will heal him; I will guide him and restore comfort to him ... Peace, peace, to those far and near," says the LORD. "And I will heal them"' (Is. 57:18–19). Paul takes 'those far' to be the Gentiles whom God wants to draw to himself and heal. Even though *God chose Israel*, he still desires to save the whole world.

Questions
1. What practical steps can we take to learn about the Old Testament and Jewish roots of the Christian faith?
2. God reaches out to those 'far away' to bring them near. Should we do the same? Who are the 'far away' we should seek, and how should we do it?
3. Why is it 'the blood of Christ' which has brought us 'near'?

Circumcision

The Old Testament law of circumcision is given in Genesis 17:9–14, and mentioned many times in the Old Testament. Circumcision was practised by many people in the ancient world, but in Israel it was given very special meaning. On the eighth day of life, male children had their 'foreskin' cut off, the loose skin on the end of the penis, as 'the sign of the covenant between me and you', as God puts it to Abraham in Genesis 17:11.

So circumcision symbolized the special relationship that Israel had with God, resting on the 'covenant', God's promise 'to be your God and the God of your descendants after you' (Gen. 17:7). This is why Paul connects circumcision so closely with 'the covenants of the promise' here in Ephesians (2:12). Not having this 'covenant' relationship with God, Gentiles were often called 'the uncircumcised' by Jews – even though in fact many of them may have been physically circumcised, for cultural or other reasons.

Because it was about a *relationship* with God, right from the start Moses told Israel that it must not be just an outward, physical mark. He told them to 'circumcise your hearts!' (Deut. 10:16), and when Israel fell into sin Jeremiah called them 'uncircumcised in heart' (Jer. 9:26). Both Stephen (Acts 7:51) and Paul (Rom. 2:28–29) repeat this charge in the New Testament.

What excites Paul so much is that this distinction between the circumcised and the uncircumcised, so fundamental to the Old Testament, has now been broken down by God in Christ. Gentiles and Jews have been made 'one new man' together (Eph. 2:15), because in Christ their hearts are *really* made new, by the Holy Spirit (Eph. 4:22–24). So Paul says about *the church of Jesus Christ*, 'we are the circumcision, we who worship by the Spirit of God!' (Phil. 3:3). And he tells the Colossians, 'in him you were also circumcised, in the putting off of the sinful nature, not with a circumcision done by the hands of men but with the circumcision done by Christ, having been buried with him in baptism and raised with him through your faith in the power of God, who raised him from the dead' (Col. 2:11–12). This *spiritual* circumcision is now symbolized by *baptism*, for both Jewish and Gentile Christians.

Ephesians 2:14–18

A completely new species

Paul explains God's new creation: Gentiles and Jews have been merged into 'one new person', reconciled to God through the cross of Christ.

Paul leaves things a little unclear at the end of verse 13. What does 'brought near' mean?

● Does it mean *brought near to God* – reconciled to him spiritually?

● Or does it mean *brought near to Israel* – brought into fellowship and sympathy with the people who bear 'the covenants of promise'?

This is a question of great importance. In Paul's day, opinions divided strongly here. There were Gentile Christians who supported the first viewpoint, and said that Israel had now lost her place as God's chosen people, so Jews would basically have to give up being Jews and become Gentiles if they wanted to belong to Christ.

On the other hand there were Jewish Christians who insisted that Jesus was the Messiah of Israel, first and foremost, and so Gentile Christians should at least respect Israel's privileged position in God's plan, if not actually become Jews.

Today, many *Gentile* Christians support this second viewpoint, and encourage all Christians to stand alongside Israel and support her in whatever ways we can.

This paragraph in Ephesians is one of Paul's responses to this disagreement. He also tackles it at length in Romans 9–11, and in *Israel in God's Plan*, p. 73 we will compare what he says there with his message here. What does he say here? He makes five points:

Christ has 'destroyed the barrier' between Jews and Gentiles (verse 14). The age-long barrier, which God himself had put up at first, simply by choosing Israel as his people, has now been broken down. The distinction between Israel and the Gentiles no longer exists (see Rom. 3:22–23, 29–30; 10:12–13). By referring to 'the dividing wall', Paul *may* have in mind the wall that stood in the Temple in Jerusalem between the Court of the Gentiles and the inner courts. Even if he is not thinking of it, it illustrates his meaning well. The 'Court of the Gentiles' had this name because Gentiles were not allowed to go any further into the Temple, and on the wall beside the gate leading to the inner courts stood a sign: 'Any man of another race entering these courts will only have himself to blame that his death follows!'

Gentiles *knew* that they had no access to the God of Israel. But now that barrier has gone – in Christ!

Christ has 'abolished the law' (verse 15a). The *Jewish law* was called a 'wall' by some Jews, because they pictured it as *protecting them* from Gentile wickedness. The law was the focus of the distinction between Israel and the Gentiles, because all the things that *made Israel different* were commanded by the law: circumcision, the festivals and the worship, the food laws, etc. But Paul does not hesitate. 'Christ has abolished the law, with its commandments and regulations!' It may have been given by God, but it's *gone*!

We need to ask exactly what Paul means by this. He seems to contradict what he says in Romans 3:31 when he asks 'Do we nullify [abolish] the law by this faith?' (using exactly the same word as in Eph. 2:15), and then replies 'Not at all! Rather, we uphold the law'. In fact he seems to contradict himself even within Ephesians, because he quotes from the Old Testament several times in the letter, and in particular quotes one of the Ten Commandments – the heart of the law – in 6:2–3, as if it had *not* been abolished.

The answer is that *the law remains as the revelation of God's will, but not as the exclusive 'mark' of one chosen people*. So all the parts of the law which *made Israel different* – the 'commandments and regulations' – have been abolished, because the distinction between Israel and the Gentiles is no more!

Christ has created 'one new person' in place of the two, Jews and Gentiles (verse 15b). In verse 10 Paul described each of us individually as 'created in Christ Jesus'. Now he pictures the whole church as a new creation. It's almost as though God was going back to the drawing-board and making a new 'Adam' to start off a whole new creation. At any rate, a new *species* emerges. The world has not seen anything like it before, because this new species – the church – is formed as that age-long barrier crashes to the ground, and Jews and Gentiles become together just *Christians*.

Christ has done this through his cross (verses 16–17). He 'has reconciled both of them to God through the cross, by which he put to death their hostility' (verse 16). Paul does not just mean their hostility to God, but also their hostility to each other. Why does the cross achieve this? Because it deals with the one problem which is common to all humankind, and to which no religion has an answer, not even Judaism: *the problem of death*.

Now 'flesh' has been replaced by 'Spirit' (verse 18). Joined to Christ, we have victory over death, and are joined to each other also, as we 'both have access to the Father by one Spirit' (verse 18). It's an all-round picture of reconciliation – a family reunion on a cosmic scale. Verse 18 involves all three 'persons' of the Trinity in this work. And 'by [literally, 'in'] one Spirit' seems deliberately to contrast 'in the flesh' in verse 11. Circumcision, done 'in the flesh', divides up humankind into Jews and Gentiles. Now 'in the Spirit' Jews and Gentiles are reconciled together to God.

Wow! What a passage.

Questions
1. What practical steps should we take, to show the unity between Jews and Gentiles in Christ?
2. 'Peace' is mentioned four times in this passage. Jesus *is* peace (verse 14), *makes* peace (verse 15), and *preaches* peace (verse 17). In what ways should we imitate him? Are there ever times when it is wrong to make peace?
3. Some scholars think that Paul may have used the words of an ancient hymn in writing this passage. Can you turn it into song, or write a poem or prayer based on it?

Israel in God's Plan

At first sight, Paul seems to say something different here about Israel, compared with what he says in Romans 9–11. In fact, some experts have felt that the difference is so great, that they use this as an argument supporting the view that Ephesians is by someone other than Paul.

Here in Ephesians he seems to say that Israel no longer has a place in God's plan: God has merged Israel and the Gentiles, abolishing the spiritual difference, and creating *one new* people of God, that is, the church of Jesus Christ.

This seems similar to what he says (in different words) in Romans 4, where he writes about Abraham. Who may claim to have Abraham as their 'father'? he asks. His answer: *all who believe in Christ*, whether they are Jews or Gentiles. 'He is the father of all who believe but have not been circumcised ... And he is also the father of the circumcised who not only are circumcised but who also walk in the footsteps of the faith that our father Abraham had ...' (Rom. 4:11–12). So Gentile Christians have as much right to call Abraham their father as Jews, and Jews who do *not* believe in Christ have *no* right to call Abraham 'father', because they are not 'walking in his footsteps'.

In Romans 11, however, he seems to say something different. There he tackles the question, 'Has God rejected his people?' (11:1 – referring to Israel, of course). His answer is 'By no means!', and then he develops a line of argument which reaches a climax in 11:25–29: 'Israel has experienced a hardening in part until the full number of the Gentiles has come in. And so all Israel will be saved! ... As far as the gospel is concerned, they are enemies on your account; but as far as election is concerned, they are loved on account of the patriarchs, for God's gifts and his call are irrevocable'.

Not only does Paul call Israel's position 'irrevocable', which seems very different from Ephesians 2, but also Romans 11 hardly pictures *reconciliation* between Jews and Gentiles. The Jews are 'enemies on your account'!

I believe that the answer to this difficulty lies in Romans 11, rather than in Ephesians 2. The Bible student who wants to tackle this question is in for an exciting but difficult journey, following

Paul through the argument of Romans 9–11. (Part of the problem is that people tend just to look at Romans 11, and don't interpret it as part of the long argument that runs right through Romans 9–11.) We can't deal with it in this short section here! Suffice it to say:

- I don't believe that there is a contradiction between Romans 11 and Ephesians 2.

- Part of the answer lies in discovering what Paul means by 'Israel' in Romans 11:25–26. Notice the way in which he *re-assigns the name* in Romans 9:6–8, in much the same way as he *re-assigns the name 'Abraham'* in Romans 4:11–12. Who may rightly call themselves 'Israel'?

- Paul was as keen as any to recognize that Israel still exists, as a *nation* and *religion* in continuity with the Old Testament people of God, and he believed the Gospel was 'first for the Jew, then for the Gentile' (Rom. 1:16). We ought to imitate his sense of priority, I believe.

I have written a small book on Romans 9–11, called *Israel in the Plan of God* (IVP, 1989), where I tackle all these questions in detail.

Ephesians 2:19–22

The real Temple!

Paul summarizes the status of the Ephesian Christians. They are God's *people*, his *family*, and the *Temple* in which he lives. The same is true for us.

The two spiritual X-rays in chapter 2 reach a marvellous climax in these verses. Paul wants to enable the Ephesians to *see themselves*. They would never have dreamed that they looked like this!

Paul uses three pictures to describe what the Ephesians now are, in Christ – two small pictures in verse 19, and then a larger one in verses 20–22.

1. 'You are no longer foreigners and aliens, but *fellow-citizens* with God's people' (verse 19). This is a *political* picture. Matching their 'exclusion from citizenship' (verse 12), they have now been made citizens of the people of God. But this 'people of God' is not *Israel*, but *the church*. (Actually Paul says 'saints' here, his usual expression for Christians – see also 1:1, 1:15, 3:18). So once again we see how Paul casts the *church* in the role of *Israel*.

2. 'You are ... members of God's household' (verse 19). This is a *domestic* picture. How dramatic! It follows on from verse 18: because we 'have access to the Father by one Spirit', Paul can actually picture us as *members of God's family*, able to have instant and intimate access to him. This leads straight into Paul's main picture here:

3. 'You are ... a holy temple in the Lord' (verses 20–22). To be members of God's family means *living in the same 'house'* as him: so from the thought 'God's household' in verse 19 Paul develops

the idea of the Temple in verses 20–22. We can pick out the main features of this most inspiring picture, as follows:

- *Its foundation is 'the apostles and prophets'* (verse 20a). Paul means the New Testament prophets, not the Old Testament ones (see 1 Cor. 12:28; Eph. 3:5; 4:11). In 3:2–6 he will explain what he means by making the apostles and prophets the foundation of the church.

- *Jesus is the 'chief cornerstone'* (verse 20b). Paul uses an architectural word here! It *either* means the stone at the corner, which was very carefully shaped and placed because it would set the 'line' of the whole wall, *or* the 'cornerstone' was actually the 'capstone', the stone at the *top* of the building which completes and makes sense of the whole wall or arch. Both meanings are helpful: the whole building *focuses on Jesus*.

- *The building is still under construction* (verses 21–22). It 'is being joined together' and 'is rising to become a holy temple' (these translations would be more accurate). As part of this growing building, 'you too are being built together ...'. All their present experiences are part of the construction process.

- *God will live in this Temple, by his Spirit* (verse 22). When Solomon finished building the first Temple in Jerusalem, it was filled with a cloud which symbolized the glory of the Lord, taking up residence in this 'magnificent temple ... a place for you to dwell for ever!' (1 Kings 8:11–12). This temple too will become 'a dwelling in which God lives by his Spirit' (verse 22).

This picture of the Temple would have spoken very powerfully to the Ephesian Christians. If they were Jewish, they would have been reminded of the Temple in Jerusalem, and of their belief as Jews that God dwelt there. No, Paul is saying: not in Jerusalem, but in *you*!

But the majority of the Ephesian Christians were Gentiles. And *they* would certainly have been reminded of the massive temple of Artemis in Ephesus. It is as though Paul is saying to them: 'Where's the temple in Ephesus? You may be tempted to answer, Right there in the centre of the city, that huge building, you can't miss it! But let me tell you, the *real* temple in Ephesus is no stone monstrosity dedicated to a devilish deity with multiple breasts. It's *you*, who are being shaped into a structure which God himself can occupy by his Spirit – the real God dwells in the real Temple, and that is *you!*'

Had any of the Ephesians heard anything like this before? We do not know. But we can be sure that it was a deep encouragement to them as they faced the daily pressure of that pagan religion on their lives. In particular, I can imagine that it encouraged their *worship*, because worship is what temples are for! Perhaps we can see now another reason why Paul lays such emphasis on worship in this letter.

Questions
1. What are the privileges that come to us as members of the family of God himself?
2. Elsewhere Paul thinks of God dwelling in each of us by his Spirit (for example, 1 Cor. 6:19), but here he thinks of *the church as a whole* becoming a place for God to live in. What do we need to do, to become churches fit for the King? What contribution could you make to the furnishings, so that your own church is fit for him to occupy?
3. 'You are no longer foreigners and aliens ...'. Does Paul's teaching here give us any guidelines for our attitude and ministry to foreigners within our society?

5

THE MAN WITH
THE CAMERA
Ephesians 3:1–13

Setting the scene

Something strange happens at the end of chapter three, verse one. Paul starts writing but then breaks off to say something else. He comes back to his original train of thought in verse 14, where he repeats 'for this reason' and then prays for the Ephesians – yet again!

So it looks as though the first thought in his mind, after the marvellous spiritual X-rays of chapter two, was to respond with prayer. In fact, he wants to pray the very thing which we were surprised *not* to find in 2:8–10 (see above, p. 58): that the Ephesians may *know God's power* for themselves.

But just as he sets off to pray this prayer, a different thought occurs to him and he breaks off to talk about *himself* (3:2–13). Why? I can think of two reasons:

- What he is going to pray for them, in 3:14–19, is really very extraordinary and probably very different from the prayers they were praying for themselves! – as we shall see when we get there. He needs to prepare them so that they are ready to pray that prayer with him. And 3:2–13 lays that foundation.

- He has just painted two amazing portraits of the Ephesians, as *risen with Christ* and *built into the new temple of God*, the church. What guarantee can the Ephesians have, that he is not simply dreaming all this up, playing with words that have no substance? It suddenly strikes Paul that, perhaps, not all his readers know *his qualifications*: and so he pauses to describe himself, *The Man with the X-ray Camera*.

Chapter 3:1–13 falls basically into two long sentences, verses 1–7 (106 words), and verses 8–12 (82 words), followed by one short concluding sentence in verse 13. This is why I have divided it into sections of such unequal length for study. The translations divide Paul's sentences differently. For instance, the NIV divides verses 1–7 into five sentences, and puts in paragraph divisions after verses 1 and 6! But we will follow the way Paul actually wrote it. In fact, verse 13 deserves a whole section to itself.

The two long sentences cover the same ground, describing the unique privilege given to Paul, first to *receive* and then to *communicate* the revelation of 'the mystery of Christ' (verses 4, 9).

81

Ephesians 3:1–7

Paul hears the secret

Paul speaks of the fantastic privilege ('grace') given to him, to be the one chosen to receive the revelation of 'the mystery' he has been describing in Ephesians so far.

Paul liked introducing himself by name into his letters, at points where he really wanted to rub a point home (see Gal. 5:2; 2 Cor. 10:1; Philem. 19). Here he does it, at first, to emphasize the importance of the prayer he is about to pray. But then he realizes that maybe his readers need to know more about him than just be reminded of his name! So he gives them his spiritual pedigree.

He describes an enormous privilege, in verses 2–7. On the strength of lesser claims than this, others have made millions, run fleets of Rolls-Royces, demanded extravagant gestures of loyalty from their devoted followers, and turned themselves almost into gods on earth. But not Paul. He is just 'the prisoner of Christ Jesus' (verse 1) – nothing more. But what a prisoner!

He describes the 'grace' he has received – that is, an enormous privilege given simply because of God's love for him. Compare verses 2 and 7 with each other: he begins and ends this long sentence by underlining the 'grace' which God has given him. He has not deserved it in the least. But God decided to make Paul the channel of a completely new revelation – not for his own sake or glory, but 'for you', his Gentile readers (verse 2).

When he describes this gift of grace in verse 7, he uses words which he last used in 1:19 when talking about the resurrection of Jesus: 'through the working of his power'. The same power of God which raised Jesus from the dead also made Paul an apostle. Paul is thinking of his experience of God's power on the road to Damascus, when he met the risen Christ in his glory, and the *moment of his conversion* became also the *moment of his appointment* to be the apostle to the Gentiles (see Acts 9:15–16).

He describes the revelation he has received In verse 3 he describes the *fact* of the revelation, in verse 6 he describes its *content*. He calls it a 'mystery', which is a word he uses elsewhere when thinking of something which is both *revealed* and *secret*:

- It could be something we have been told about, but have not yet experienced, so it is still a future 'mystery' (for example, Rom. 11:25; 1 Cor. 15:51).

- Or it could be something we have been told about, but which is too great for us to understand fully (for example, Col. 2:2–3).

- Or it could be something we have been told about, but which *was* kept secret for a long time and not revealed to others (for example, Rom. 16:25–26; Col. 1:26, and here).

Verse 6 is a beautiful summary of the message of 2:11–22. When Paul says, 'As I have already written briefly' in verse 3, he is probably referring to everything he has already written in the letter. He has been unpacking 'the mystery made known to me by revelation' (verse 3).

He describes his partnership with others He does not claim exclusive rights to this revelation! It was kept secret from other generations, but 'has now been revealed by the Spirit to God's holy apostles and prophets' (verse 5). Paul doesn't actually mention that he is one of these 'holy apostles'. We have to remember that from 1:1! Verse 5 is not in contradiction to verse 3. We can see from his letter to the Galatians how keen Paul was to say *both* that God had revealed the Gospel to him, *and* that God had also revealed *the same Gospel* to the other apostles (see Gal. 1:1 – 2:10).

But he is not just in partnership with the other apostles and prophets. He is also in partnership with us, his readers! Verse 4 tells all. It is essential that people should be able to *recognize* that Paul really has received a revelation from God! Otherwise – what's the point of it? A revelation received in lonely isolation and never recognized or received by anyone else is really no revelation at all. Paul is the Man with the X-ray Camera, but X-ray pictures can do no good if the patient refuses to believe that the broken bone on the screen is really his!

Now we see why Paul prays that the *Ephesians also* will have 'the Spirit of wisdom and revelation' (1:17). The same Spirit who gave the revelation to the 'apostles and prophets' will help them to see that it *is* revelation.

Questions

1. Who were the 'holy apostles and prophets'? Do you think that God still speaks in the same way to prophets today as he did through prophets in New Testament times?
2. What makes *you* feel that in chapters 1 and 2 Paul really does show 'insight into the mystery of Christ'? Or do you have doubts about it?
3. Paul calls himself 'a servant of this gospel' (verse 7). Should all Christians be 'servants of the gospel' or is that a special calling? How could we 'serve' the gospel?

Paul in prison

Paul spent several periods of time in prison. We read about four imprisonments in Acts – in Philippi (Acts 16:23), in Jerusalem (Acts 22:29), in Caesarea (Acts 23:33–35) and in Rome (Acts 28:30), but he refers to 'frequent' imprisonments in 2 Corinthians 11:23, which was written before three of these!

It was not nice being a prisoner. Quite apart from the physical discomfort, there was the social disgrace to bear. When we look at verse 13, we will see how Paul coped with this himself. But others found it difficult, too. In Philippians Paul mentions some Christians who were plainly embarrassed at being associated with a prisoner, and wanted to distance themselves from him (Phil. 1:12–18). Having your apostle imprisoned was a test of loyalty for many Christians. If they went on supporting him, part of his 'disgrace' would rub off on them. And this was a very practical issue, for in those days prisoners depended on their friends to feed them (as also in many countries today: see 2 Timothy 1:16).

So Paul makes sure that the Ephesians know where he is. He announces his imprisonment with a fanfare of trumpets! – and tells them firmly that it is 'for the sake of you Gentiles' (verse 1).

Actually there is more than meets the eye in 'the prisoner of Christ Jesus'. Yes, Paul means that he has been imprisoned *because of* Christ Jesus for preaching the Gospel. But the phrase also means 'imprisoned *by* Christ Jesus', and Paul probably has this in mind, too. He is *held captive* by the Lord Jesus, *bound* to follow and serve him. This comes across even more clearly in Ephesians 4:1, where he calls himself a 'prisoner in the Lord' (literal translation). See also Philemon 1:9. So his *physical* imprisonment is merely the result of his *spiritual* imprisonment, to Christ – something much more important.

Ephesians was probably written during Paul's imprisonment in Rome. At this point, he had been held *without charge*, and without being brought to trial, for well over two years. We might have expected the Apostle to the Gentiles, called 'to preach the gospel where Christ was not known' (Rom. 15:20), to feel slightly frustrated about this state of affairs! How could he fulfil his calling under these circumstances? But there is no sign at all that he felt bitter or resentful. Why? We shall begin to find the answer, and get a glimpse into how he *did* feel about it, when we look at 3:13.

Ephesians 3:8–12

Paul tells the secret

Paul says some surprising things about preaching the Gospel. It's not just travelling around talking to people. It's being what God has made us, in Christ.

In these verses Paul moves on from *receiving* to *communicating* the 'mystery'. Again he mentions the 'grace' given to him (verse 8), but this time it is 'to preach to the Gentiles the unsearchable riches of Christ, and to make plain to everyone the administration of this mystery'. This was how he literally *spent* his life: see 2 Corinthians 11:23–33 for what it meant for Paul to preach 'the riches of Christ' to the Gentiles.

'The administration of this mystery': this seems a strange way to describe the Gospel. Paul has used this rather unusual word 'administration' before, in 1:10, where the NIV translates it 'to be put into effect'. A literal translation there would be, 'for the administration of the fulness of the times'. This 'administration' of world history was part of 'the mystery of his will' which God has 'made known to us' (1:9). So now Paul goes around, preaching 'the unsearchable riches of Christ'. But these 'riches' do not just contain good news about the forgiveness of sins and new life in Christ. They *also* contain good news about God's overall plan for the world, in particular about how he plans 'to bring all things in heaven and earth together under one head, even Christ', which is how Paul puts it in 1:10.

Paul has just been talking about one way in which this overall plan has started to work. All things under one head, even Christ? God is working towards this by bringing together Jews and Gentiles, uniting them 'in one body' in Christ. Already, in the church, we can see something of what God plans for the whole world, as this dreadful racial barrier is broken down and a whole 'new being' is born (2:15).

So 'the administration of this mystery' probably means something like 'how God is going to achieve his special Plan'.

This all helps us to understand verse 10, which is quite a challenge to interpret. Before reading on, why not pause and think carefully about this verse. What exactly is Paul saying? Who are these 'rulers and authorities'? How do they hear 'the manifold wisdom of God'? (Paul says, 'through the church' – but does the church *speak* to these 'rulers', or what?)

The experts have different views about all these questions, and it would be too complicated to set out all the varieties. So I must make it clear that what follows is just my own view!

● We met these 'rulers and authorities' before in 1:21. There it was clear that these are *spiritual powers of evil*, over which Jesus is now supreme and victorious.

● Maybe we can say a little more about them. Some people have wondered whether these 'powers' are attached to particular nations or countries. Daniel meets the angel of *Babylon*, who tells him that he has been at war with the angel of Persia, and refers also to the angel of Greece, and Michael, the angel of Israel (Dan. 10:12–21; 12:1). It certainly makes sense if these 'rulers and authorities' represent different nations – at any rate, if this is *part* of their meaning:

● For *the church* shows them that they have been defeated, their power taken away. The greatest racial barrier of all, that between Jews and Gentiles, has been destroyed. And so, potentially, *all national and racial distinctions have been undermined*.

● The church proclaims the overthrow of these 'rulers' *just by its very existence*. For it is composed of men and women from every nation on earth, who are united in Christ without distinction. 'You are worthy to take the scroll and to open its seals', cry the elders before the Lamb, 'because you were slain, and with your blood you purchased people for God from every tribe and language and people and nation!' (Rev. 5:9). The *international* church of Jesus Christ testifies to God's 'administration of the mystery'. Praise him!

- The church shows God's 'manifold wisdom' to the 'rulers'. The word 'manifold' means literally 'many-coloured'. In Britain you can go into a Garden Centre and buy a packet of 'variegated' seeds, which means that when they come up, the flowers will be of different colours, making a beautiful, varied display. God's 'variegated wisdom' is shown by a church in which people of different backgrounds, races, abilities, types, yes even *colours* are all made one in Christ, and so *demonstrate* the overthrow of the 'powers' which try to divide up humankind into rival groups and races.

Questions

1. Should your church be doing more to 'demonstrate' that all racial and other barriers have been broken down in Christ? Think about your own local church, and the church nationally and world-wide.

2. What *practical* steps can we take, when the barriers and distinctions maintained by the world around us seem to be *preserved* in the church, and not broken down?

3. In verse 8 Paul says 'I am less than the least of *all* God's people'. Why does he say this? Is he being honest here? Should we *all* say the same thing about ourselves, or not? (See 1 Tim. 1:12–15; 1 Cor. 15:9–10.)

'Heavenly realms' – what and where?

The phrase 'in the heavenly realms' comes five times in Ephesians:

- It is where God has 'blessed' us in Christ (1:3)

- It is where Christ has been seated at God's right hand, 'far above' all the rulers and authorities (1:20–21)

- It is where we too have been seated with Christ because of the resurrection (2:6)

- It is where the church shows God's wisdom to the rulers and authorities (3:10)

- It is where all the various 'spiritual forces of evil' are, against whom we must put on God's armour (6:12).

Paul doesn't use this phrase anywhere else in his writings, so it is a special feature of Ephesians. (The closest he comes elsewhere is in Philippians 2:10, where he uses the same word in describing the 'things in heaven' which will bow at the name of Jesus.) So where are these 'heavenly realms'?

Some writers have tried to draw a 'Map of the Universe According to Paul', and to locate an area which could be labelled 'Heavenly Realms' – perhaps the next stop after the *Air*, on the way up to *Heaven Itself* which is 'far above' where the 'powers' are? This is probably the wrong approach.

These 'heavenly realms' contain a large and very mixed gathering. *Jesus* is there, exalted in glory at God's right hand. The defeated *'powers'* are there. The *Devil* is there. *We – the church –* are there, seated with Christ, engaged in battle and showing God's wisdom to the powers. It is probably best to think of 'the heavenly realms' as *the whole spiritual side of existence, the unseen world which we inhabit just as much as the world of sense and sight around us.*

Thinking of it like this helps us to see how we can apparently be in two places at once: both here on earth, and 'seated with him in the heavenly realms in Christ Jesus' (2:6). We're not really in two places at all, because the heavenly realms 'intersect' with this world like the light which falls outside the visible spectrum. Ultra-violet light is really there and can affect us a lot. On a hot day my white skin becomes red and sore. But I can't actually *see* the light which does this to me. Similarly, we human beings live on two planes at the same time, the spiritual and the physical, each as 'real' as the other.

Generally speaking, Western cultures have killed off awareness of the whole spiritual side of life. Third World cultures have not – though it is often the *powers of evil* which dominate people's awareness, especially in tribal religions. For Western Christians, to come alive in Christ often means becoming aware for the first time of the whole spiritual dimension to human existence. In the East, it often means finding *deliverance* from spiritual forces which seemed horribly real and powerful. Whether Western or Eastern, we need to learn to *live in Christ* in both sides of our existence, earthly and heavenly.

Ephesians 3:13

Paul suffers for the secret

Paul encourages the Ephesians not to be discouraged by his imprisonment because, he says, 'My sufferings are your glory!'

Paul started off in verse 1 by calling himself 'the prisoner of Christ Jesus for the sake of you Gentiles'. Now, just before picking up the prayer which he was about to pray then, he comes back to the thought that his sufferings are 'for your sake'.

How could this be true? After all, his imprisonment *stopped* him from 'preaching to the Gentiles the unsearchable riches of Christ', which is how he describes his ministry in verse 8. How could it be 'for your sake' that he was held back from fulfilling the ministry God had given him for them?

This is such an important question. Amongst the readers of this Bible Guide, or in the groups using it to study Ephesians, there will certainly be people who feel frustrated and useless, hindered by one handicap or another from being what they think they could be, for God. 'If only ...'! In different ways we are all prisoners – in imperfect bodies, in marred personalities, in hurtful relationships, in unfulfilling jobs, in joyless churches, in oppressive regimes, in poverty, in sickness, in pain ... the list is endless. How did Paul manage to cope with the imprisonment which meant the *denial* of his calling from God? And see the section on *Paul in Prison* (p. 84): there is no sign that he ever became bitter or expressed frustration about it.

Perhaps he just means: I've been locked up for preaching the Gospel to you Gentiles, so 'for your sake' just means 'because of you'. This is true, of course. But he must mean more than this, because he actually calls his sufferings 'your glory'. Three things help us to understand Paul here:

In prison or not, *he is spiritually free.* Just look at verse 12! 'In him and through faith in him we may approach God with *freedom* and confidence'. What a word for a prisoner to use! Chained he may be physically, but spiritually there are no restrictions. Right into the presence of God, with confidence. The word 'approach' here is the same as the word he uses in 2:18: 'Through him we both have *access* to the Father by one Spirit'. Paul is not just under house-arrest in Rome. He is knocking at the throne-room door, admitted with joy into the Presence.

He says something similar in Ephesians 6:19–20. Here he twice uses the same word 'freedom', although the NIV has translated it 'fearlessly'. Paul calls himself *an ambassador for the Gospel in chains,* and asks for prayer, 'that whenever I open my mouth, words may be given me so that I will fearlessly ['with freedom'] make known the mystery of the Gospel' (6:19). He knows that he cannot just charge around speaking whenever *he* feels he should. He needs to be *given words by God,* otherwise there will be no spiritual power in what he says. If God gives him the words, then he speaks 'with freedom'. As he says to Timothy, 'God's word is not chained!' (2 Tim. 2:9).

In prison or not, *God directs his life.* God's wisdom is to be made known to the powers 'according to his eternal purpose which he accomplished in Christ Jesus' (verse 11). God has a Plan which is sure to be accomplished. *He* has decided how his wisdom is to be made known. And if this includes locking up the apostle charged with talking about it, fine! All through his ministry, Paul allowed God to direct him – although he also told God clearly what he would *like* to do: see Romans 1:10–13; 15:31–32; Acts 16:6–10; 19:21 (here Luke says that he 'decided *in the Spirit*'). As we saw above, Paul was first and foremost a prisoner *of* Christ, whether or not he was also a prisoner *for* Christ.

In prison or not, *he shares the sufferings of Christ for his people.* The first two points mean that he can say 'Don't be discouraged!' in verse 13. This third point is what enables him to say 'my sufferings are your glory!'

As we saw above, many would think that Paul's imprisonment brought *shame* upon them, not glory. Paul encourages Timothy, 'Do not be ashamed to testify about our Lord, or ashamed of me his prisoner' (2 Tim. 1:8). In his sufferings, Paul is a constant reminder that the Christian life is not all victory, glory and strength. It means victory, but *through* defeat, glory *through* dishonour, strength *in* weakness. That's what the cross is all about – the moment of *death* is the moment when a whole new creation is born (2:15–16)!

But it is more than this. Paul actually thought of himself as *suffering for* his Gentile churches in a way *like* the sufferings of Christ for us. In Colossians 1:24 he even says, 'I rejoice in what was suffered for you, and I fill up in my flesh what is still lacking in regard to Christ's afflictions, for the sake of his body, which is the church'. Of course he did not think of himself as *bearing their sin*: only Jesus could do that (Rom. 3:25). But Paul could *stand alongside* his Lord and play his part, sharing the suffering of his Lord for the sake of his people. See also 2 Corinthians 1:3–7, 4:11–12; 2 Timothy 2:10.

Questions
1. Do you think that we can 'share the sufferings of Christ' in the same way as Paul, or was that something only he could do? See also 1 Peter 4:12–16.
2. What encouragement does Paul give us here, as we face our own 'imprisonments', whatever they are?
3. Some parts of the church world-wide are called to face suffering more than others. What can we do to express our fellowship with them in Christ?

PRAYER FOCUS 2
Ephesians 3:14–21

Setting the scene

In 3:14 Paul resumes the train of thought he broke off in 3:1 – and continues with the *prayer* he was starting at that point. And what a prayer it is! This prayer is unique in the New Testament, for the *passionate love* that motivates it, the *sparkling theology* that inspires it, and the *profound worship* that undergirds it. We will see all these things as we study it.

It falls into two parts. First, a prayer for the Ephesians in verses 14–19, and then a 'doxology', or *outburst of praise* in verses 20–21. The worship which has never been far below the surface bubbles up again and brings the first half of the letter to a glorious conclusion.

The prayer in verses 14–19 is all one sentence again in the original (this time of 86 words). But it doesn't just come tumbling out with no thought. Paul has shaped this prayer beautifully:

1. Verses 14–15, opening description of God (this is always a good way to begin prayer!)

2. Verses 16–17a, first request, in two parts:

   ● that they may be strengthened within (verse 16)

   ● that Christ may dwell in their hearts (verse 17a)

3. Verses 17b–19a, second request, in two parts:

   ● that they may be able to 'grasp how wide and long ...' (verse 18)

   ● that they may know the love of Christ that passes knowledge (verse 19a)

4. Verse 19b, third request, amazingly bold, summing the others up: that they may be filled with all the fulness of God.

Notice how the first request focuses on *strength*, the second on *knowledge*. And notice how, in both requests, the first part looks straight at the Ephesians, and the second part introduces Christ as the answer to their need.

Ephesians 3:14–17a

Prayer for power

As Paul prays for the Ephesians, he lets them see that *inner* strength is their most vital need. The same is true for us.

In this section we look at the introduction to the prayer, and the first request.

'I bend my knees before the Father ...', writes Paul (literal translation). He does not, of course, mean that he actually goes down on his knees while writing. He is reporting a prayer he frequently prays. 'I bend my knees' sounds like a fairly ordinary way to describe a prayer, but in fact it is quite unusual. Jews and Christians generally *stood* to pray, with hands and faces raised (see Mark 11:25; Matt. 6:5). *Kneeling* to pray was a sign of a special occasion (for example 1 Chron. 29:20), or of special urgency (Acts 9:40) or of special emotion (Luke 22:41; Acts 20:36), or just of sheer worship and adoration (Rom. 14:11; Phil 2:10). So just by saying 'I kneel' Paul expresses the depth of his love and concern for the Ephesians – and also his deep reverence for the God to whom he prays.

He calls this God 'the Father from whom every family in heaven and on earth is named'. This translation is a little different from the NIV, which has 'his whole family' rather than 'every family'. (The reasons for preferring 'every family' are explained in *Every Family*, p. 98.) Paul's thought is that God is the supreme *Father*, who has organized the whole universe, both heaven and earth, into family groups. This means that

- he has absolute authority over the whole universe, and

- he is the best kind of Father, caring and providing the very best for his children.

On this basis, Paul prays. He knows that nothing can hinder God from giving the Ephesian Christians the very best: he lacks neither the *power* nor the *will* to meet their needs.

His prayer in verses 16–17a is that 'out of his glorious riches he may strengthen you with power through his Spirit in your inner being, so that Christ may dwell in your hearts through faith'. He returns to the theme of *power* which was so important in the first Prayer Focus in 1:15–23. In fact we have been expecting him to come back to this theme. The Ephesian Christians knew their need for power only too well. They must have been deeply encouraged to hear that Jesus is now supreme over all other powers (1:19–21). But, even though Paul has revealed so much about what God has done for them in Christ, he has not yet shown them how God's power can be a real, living, daily experience for them, facing a hostile society ready to summon up demonic powers against them.

In fact that is what Paul will do in the second half of the letter. There he will explain how they can live by the power of God. But here he *prays* for that power for them – and in a most surprising way.

It is not hard to imagine what *kind* of power they felt that they needed: power to combat the armies of the Devil, the 'spiritual forces of evil in the heavenly realms' (6:12), to ward off spells and perhaps even to go on the offensive, breaking down strongholds of evil, throwing back the powers of evil by the sword of the Spirit. The Kingdom of God on the march!

But this is *not* the power for which Paul prays. He wants *inner* strength for them. The front line of the battle is not 'out there', but 'in here', deep in their 'inner being'. That is where they need to win victories, by the Spirit. And that is not all. If the Spirit of God will strengthen them inwardly in this way, then they will be fit and strong to receive Christ, who will come and 'dwell' in them (verse 17).

Notice that Paul does not assume that Christ *already* 'dwells' in their hearts. That is a goal for which he prays, and for which they must long. They need inner strength – but not, in the end, so that they may be protected from the powers of evil. The walls of their hearts need to be strong so that they will not buckle under the strain of containing the Christ within them! What an ambition to have.

Questions
1. What surprises you about this prayer of Paul? And why?
2. Is this 'inner being' strength something that each of us should seek individually, or is it something that a church can have? Or both? Which is more important? And how, *practically*, should we seek to have this strength?
3. Paul often writes about us being 'in' Christ, but only rarely about Christ being 'in' us. Apart from Ephesians 3:17, see Romans 8:10, Colossians 1:27. Why do you think this is?

Every family

'... from whom his whole family in heaven and on earth derives its name ...' (verse 15).

I suggested above that the NIV translation of the phrase 'his whole family' is wrong, and that it should be 'every family'. The NIV makes it refer to the universal church, the family of God in heaven and earth. This is much easier to understand than the translation 'every family'. It is easy to see how the church, God's family, gets its name from him. But what about 'every family in heaven and on earth'? How can a completely godless family, full of hatred and strife, 'derive its name' from God? And in any case, what are the 'families in heaven' to which this translation refers?

So it is easy to see why the NIV prefers 'his whole family'. The trouble is that 'every family' is a much better translation of Paul's Greek. To begin with, there is no 'his' in the Greek. There is no 'the' in the Greek, either, which makes the translation 'the whole family' impossible. Without 'the', the phrase is general and not specific, and most naturally means 'every family'.

But how could we make sense of this? In Greek the word 'family' is *patria*, which is closely related to the word for 'father', *pater*. It is as though, in English, our word was not 'family' but 'fathery'. So, in a quite literal sense, every family is *named* by 'the father'. The name is a related version of the same word.

But Paul must mean more than this. He can't be simply giving us a language-lesson. There must be more to God 'naming' every family in heaven and on earth than just an accident of the Greek language. In the Bible, to 'name' something means (a) to show your power over it, and (b) to give it its nature, or at least to express something important about its nature. In the Bible, names carried meanings, and often said something about the bearer. Eli's daughter-in-law called her baby 'Ichabod', literally 'No-glory!' when she heard the news that the ark had been captured (1 Sam. 4:21–22). Isaiah had to give his son an extraordinary name which was actually a message to Israel: the name turned the poor boy into a walking *sign* of God's judgment on Israel (Isaiah 8:3–4, 18; see also Hos. 1:3 – 2:1).

God has 'named' all the families in heaven and earth by *giving them their nature*. Families are all about *relationships*. They bring people together, remind us that we belong with others, that we cannot live on our own, that we need to take responsibility for each other and depend deeply on each other. Of course it can all go horribly wrong. Relationships can become very hurtful. Children can be dreadfully damaged by the very people who should care for them. But we recognize that it is not the fault of *the family as such* that things go wrong. It is *our* fault, our failure to live together as we should.

So Paul begins this prayer by reminding us that *God has structured heaven and earth so that all their inhabitants live together in family groupings – for good or ill*. He has made us *social* beings, that is, beings who need relationships in order to be at peace and grow. This is because he himself is 'the Father' – a *social* title. And we know what the *society* is, to which 'the Father' belongs. He belongs in relationship with 'the Son' and with 'the Spirit' – a unique society, of love and mutual dependence.

In this sense, *every* family is 'named' by God the Father, even when it does not acknowledge him or breaks up in hurt and hatred. We are made in his image, made to love and depend upon each other. And Paul seems to be thinking of the various families of angels, both good and evil, which inhabit heaven, as well as all the families of earth.

This is a beautiful way to introduce the prayer, because the prayer is all about *the growth of our relationships, both with God (Father, Son and Holy Spirit), and with each other*.

Ephesians 3:17b–19a

Prayer for knowledge

We need to be strong, as Christians. But why? Above all, so that we can grow in our understanding and experience of God and of Christ. That's why!

I wonder whether the Ephesians were surprised by this second request even more than by the first. Again the prayer focuses on *power*: 'that you ... may have power' (verse 18). But again, the power is applied to something other than external 'spiritual warfare' against the forces of evil. 'I pray that you, being rooted and established in love, may have power, together with all the saints, to *grasp* ... and to *know* ...' (author's italics). Their greatest need is not to be equipped with a battery of spiritual weapons to strike down Satan and his forces, but to *grow* in *knowledge*. I am sure that the Ephesians were not ignorant, uninstructed Christians. Their faith and love had already grown (1:15). And so I am also fairly sure that they would *not* have listed knowledge as Need Number One. But that is where Paul puts his finger. What exactly does he pray?

He prays that love may be their foundation (verse 17). Throughout this prayer Paul uses 'building' pictures. Or more accurately, he uses 'Temple' pictures, following on from his description of the church as a Temple in 2:20–22. He has already prayed that Christ might 'dwell' in their hearts (verse 17). Now he prays that their *foundation* might be love (the word translated 'established' is literally 'founded' – the same word as in 2:20). And in verses 18 and 19 further 'Temple' pictures appear.

In 2:20, the apostles and prophets were the foundation of the Temple. There is no contradiction, that here the foundation is *love*.

Paul is thinking of a different kind of foundation. The point is: *they cannot grow in knowledge on their own.* They can only do so 'together with all the saints' (verse 18), that is, *in conscious fellowship with the whole church of Jesus Christ.* So the foundation of this growth in knowledge will be *love,* because this binds the church together. They need to put down roots into that love, so that their commitment to the rest of the church is unshakeable.

He prays that they may grasp 'what is the breadth and the length and the height and the depth' (verse 18). This is a literal translation. Paul does not actually mention 'the love of Christ' in verse 18. The NIV has brought this forward from the next verse – because the obvious question is, 'Breadth, length, height and depth *of what?*'

The NIV may be right: he wants them to grasp the true dimensions of the love of Christ. But it could be other things:

● These may be the dimensions of the *universe.* Some magic spells used these words with this meaning.

● Or they could be the dimensions of *the wisdom of God,* which is described in Job 11:8–9 as 'higher than the heavens ... deeper than the depths of the grave ... longer than the earth and wider than the sea'.

● Or they could be the dimensions of *the Temple.* Ezekiel measured the Temple he saw in vision, to discover how perfect it was (Ezek. 40–43). Zechariah saw *Jerusalem* being measured (Zech. 2:1–2). John was told to measure the Temple (Rev. 11:1–2). The heavenly city (= Temple), coming down from heaven, is a perfect cube with perfect dimensions (Rev. 21:15–17).

I am most drawn to this last interpretation, because it fits with the 'Temple' idea here in Ephesians. Paul longs that they might *truly* and *fully* grasp what it means to belong to the new creation, the church of Jesus Christ, the Temple of which he is the cornerstone.

He prays that they might know the unknowable – the love of Christ (verse 19). Love is the foundation of this building. And it rests not on a vague, general 'love', but on *the love of Christ.* We could put it like this (though Paul may not have precisely this thought in mind): the most important dimension of this building is the fourth one, 'depth', because the whole building will be insecure unless it rests on solid foundations. And foundations, as any surveyor will tell you, are the hardest part of a building to measure and map. How are they constructed? How far down do they go?

In the case of this spiritual building, they 'surpass knowledge'. We can *know* the love of Christ, but never *know it fully*. There will always be further aspects to discover and 'map'. This is because the love of Christ is the *fundamental fact* of God's whole relationship to the world.

- Jesus Christ his Son is 'the One he loves' (Eph. 1:6).

- God decided 'in love' that we too would be his sons 'through Jesus Christ' (1:4–5).

- God has made this much-loved Jesus Christ the *focus* and the *goal* of the universe and all its history (1:10).

- He has done this by *giving* his Son to bear our sins and our death (1:7), so that

- 'because of his great love, with which he loved us' (2:4) he might make us alive from the death of sin and unite us with himself (2:5–6).

That is a broad sketch-map of the love Paul wants us to 'know'. He wants us to know it intimately – which of course means not just in our heads, but in our whole experience. So he will tell us in the next section

- to 'bear with one another in love' (4:2),

- to 'speak the truth in love', as the whole church 'builds itself up in love' (4:15–16),

- to 'live a life of love, just as Christ loved us' (5:2), and especially

- he will tell husbands to 'love your wives, just as Christ loved the church and gave himself up for her' (5:25).

The challenge to grow in love is the fundamental challenge of the Christian life.

Questions

1. Paul says that we can only grow in knowledge 'together with all the saints'. What does this say to us about our attitude towards the beliefs of other Christians and churches which may differ from ours?

2. What practical steps should we take to see Paul's prayer answered in our own lives? How may we learn to 'grasp ... and to know'?

3. 'I love all mankind! It's people I can't stand'. Take an opportunity with others to discuss *the practical obstacles* in your church to growing in the love of Christ. You may be tempted to think that the obstacles are *other people*, so ... what should you do about it?

Ephesians 3:19b–21

Praise Be!

Prayer gives way to praise as Paul's mind and heart are filled with God, and he leads us to *worship*, our greatest privilege as human beings.

Paul's prayer reaches a climax with his final request, which sums up all the others: 'that you may be filled to the measure of all the fulness of God' (verse 19b). What does this mean?

Sometimes Paul likes teasing his readers. This is one of those occasions. He teases us by using words which seem designed to puzzle, and which certainly make us think hard. These words make great demands on us, because there are several possible meanings, and our spiritual and scriptural instincts are tested as we try to decide between them.

- We could find just a vague meaning here, for example, 'that you might fully receive everything that God wants and plans for you!' On this interpretation, 'the fulness of God' would be the fulness *he wants to give* – as in John 1:16. But this seems weak. Paul must mean much more in Colossians 1:19, where he writes about Jesus, 'God was pleased to have all his fulness dwell in him', or in Colossians 2:9, where he says 'in Christ all the fulness of the Deity lives in bodily form.'

- So perhaps *Christ* is 'the fulness of God', and Paul is praying that we may *become like him* – the supreme goal of our existence. This would fit with Paul's description of that goal in Ephesians 4:13: '... until we all reach unity in the faith and in the knowledge of the Son of God and become mature, *attaining to the whole measure of the fulness of Christ*'. But here in 3:19 Paul writes about 'the fulness of God', not 'the fulness of Christ', and we ought at least to ask if there is a difference between these.

● Another thought appeals to me. Paul has used several images and pictures associated with the Temple in this prayer – dwelling (verse 17a), foundations (verse 17b), and measuring (verse 18) – all of them picking up the description of the church as a *Temple under construction* in 2:20–22. There Paul wrote about the *ultimate purpose* of this construction – that the church should become 'a dwelling in which God lives by his Spirit' (2:22). I suggested that we should think of the Temple dedicated by Solomon, which was called 'a place for God to dwell for ever'. At that dedication we read that 'When the priests withdrew from the Holy Place, the cloud filled the temple of the LORD. And the priests could not perform their service because of the cloud, for the glory of the LORD filled his temple' (1 Kings 8:10–11).

The Lord filled his Temple! This helps us to understand Paul's prayer, I believe. He prays that the Temple *which is the church* should become fit and ready to receive the 'full' presence of God. 'Oh!' says Paul, 'that the church might be able truly to receive God, in the full awesomeness of his blazing holiness!'

There is a difference between the filling of this Temple and Solomon's Temple. In Solomon's case, the Temple was filled in a moment, when the ark was brought in. But the filling of the church of Jesus Christ is a process. The NIV brings this out nicely in its translation, 'that you may be *filled to the measure* of all the fulness of God' (author's italics). Later, Paul will tell the Ephesians to 'go on being filled with the Spirit' (5:18, literal translation): that means seeking *an ever greater fulness*. So, as the Temple is gradually built, it becomes more and more able to contain the God whose house it is.

The encouragement in 5:18 to 'be filled with the Spirit' leads straight into worship: 'Speak to one another with psalms, hymns and spiritual songs ...' (5:19). Exactly the same happens here! In 3:20–21 Paul leads us in worship. And as he does so, he enables us to praise God for the wonderful panorama of truth which he has displayed around us in chapters 1–3:

- He has focused on the theme of God's *power*, which is not something distant but is 'at work within us' (verse 20).

- He has focused on the relationship between us, the church, and Jesus Christ – in fact he has described the *union* which God has created between us and him. So *together* the church and Christ bring glory to God (3:21).

- He has focused on *prayer* as our greatest calling, as human beings – both prayer which is *praise* to God (1:3–14), and prayer which is *asking* for others (1:15–23). So now he reminds us that, before God, we 'ask and think' (verse 20: 'think' is a better translation than 'imagine').

- He has taught us that God has a plan for the whole universe and the whole of its history – to *sum it all up* in Christ. So the 'glory!' we now give him through Christ will last 'throughout all generations, for ever and ever' (verse 21).

Questions

1. Do you think that 'the fulness of God' is

   - something we should each seek, individually

   - or something each church fellowship should seek together

   - or something which can only be true of the whole universal church in the 'age to come' (2:7)?

2. What do verses 20–21 say to you about your own prayer life – both yours, and your church's?

3. We have reached the half-way point in Ephesians. In a group if possible, look back over the three chapters you have studied, and make a list under the heading, 'What God has taught me/us through Ephesians so far'.

BEING THE CHURCH
OF CHRIST
Ephesians 4:1–16

7

Setting the scene

Ephesians falls nicely into two halves – and the second half begins here at 4:1. In this respect, Ephesians is quite like Romans, which also falls into two sections overall. Romans 12:1 begins in a similar way, 'Therefore I urge you ...', and then Paul gives lots of practical instructions about living the Christian life. Romans, like Ephesians, has a first half which focuses on doctrine, *the truths of the faith* (Rom. 1–11, Eph. 1–3), and a second half which focuses on ethics, *the practice of the faith* (Rom. 12–16, Eph. 4–6).

In both cases the practical section begins with 'I urge you, therefore ...' The 'therefore' says a lot: *because* all this is true, *therefore* you must live like this. Of course, Romans 1–11 also contains practical teaching, just as Ephesians 1–3 does (see for example, Rom. 6:12–14; Eph. 2:8–10). And Romans 12–16, like Ephesians 4–6, contains some beautiful *doctrine* (see for example, Rom. 15:8–13; Eph. 4:4–10). But basically from now on we will be thinking about *the practical outworking of the teaching Paul has given so far*.

What is he going to say? A glance ahead reveals the outline:

1. *Life in the Church, Ephesians 4:1 – 5:21*. Paul has said much about the church of Jesus Christ in chapters 1–3: its origin (1:4), its Saviour (1:7), its destiny (1:12–14), its Lord (1:20–23), its relationship to God (2:4–10), its unity (2:15–19), its apostles (3:2–5), its calling (3:10), and its power (3:16–19). Now, drawing on all this, he tells us how belonging to this church must shape our lives.

2. *Life in the Family, Ephesians 5:22 – 6:9*. Paul focuses some special teaching on Christian family relationships. We will ask *why* he does this when we get there.

3. *Life in the Battle, Ephesians 6:10–20*. Paul allows no illusions about the opposition. Someone is out to kill us. But God has provided all we need for the battle.

The first part of all this, Ephesians 4:1–16, is special. Many countries have a written *Constitution* as well as *laws* to govern the life of their citizens. The Constitution sets the framework, and then the legal system is supposed to regulate the way things actually happen. For instance, the American Constitution states the 'inalienable rights' of all American citizens, and sets up the distinction between the executive, the legislature and the judiciary which is basic to the way the whole country operates. Then the laws spell out the details. Similarly here in Ephesians, 4:1–16 describes the *Constitution* of the Church of Christ, the basic framework of our lives as Christians, and then 4:17 – 6:20 gives us the down-to-earth, practical *living-out* of the Constitution – the 'laws' of the Church of Christ.

Ephesians 4:1–6

Preserving unity

Principle no. 1 in the Constitution of the Church is *unity*. Paul encourages us to work at 'keeping' it (verses 1–3), and then explains why (verses 4–6).

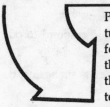

Paul begins his statement of the church's Constitution by reminding us of what he is: 'a prisoner for the Lord' (verse 1). Why does he mention this? Is he angling for their sympathy – thinking that this might make them more willing to listen? A literal translation is important here (see above, p. 85): 'a prisoner *in* the Lord'. He is a prisoner *in* the Lord, whether locked up in jail or travelling free, and the same is true for all of us. We are all *bound* to Jesus Christ, if we are members of his church. And so we are *bound* to live by the Constitution on which it is founded.

And here is the first foundation principle! We must 'walk worthy of the calling with which you have been called, with all humility and gentleness, with patience, bearing with one another in love, being very keen to preserve the unity of the Spirit in the shared bond of peace' (verses 2–3, literal translation).

By using the word 'bond' in verse 3, Paul brings out the thought that *we are all prisoners* – bound to each other, to live with each other in peace. This 'peace' rests on a unity which the Spirit has created and given to us. Here Paul looks back to 2:18–22 and his picture of the church as a new creation, a new *Temple*, in which Jews and Gentiles have been joined into one by the Spirit.

That's what God has made us by his Spirit. But though *he* has done it, *we* need to work at *preserving* the unity he has created. The Temple is under construction, not finished yet. Sadly, we can knock bits off it and start demolishing it, unless we work at unity.

When Paul pictures the church as a Temple to the Christians in Corinth, he warns them, 'If anyone destroys God's temple, God will destroy him! For that temple is sacred ...' (1 Cor. 3:17). And the Corinthians were in danger of destroying the Temple *by their disunity*: they had divided themselves into rival groups following different apostles (1 Cor. 1:12–13; 3:3–9).

In verse 2 Paul summarizes the four qualities we need to have, in order to keep unity with each other:

- *Humility*: the quality we need when others disagree with us. We may be wrong!

- *Gentleness*: the quality we need when we *know* that others are wrong and need correction.

- *Patience*: the quality we need when they fail to respond to our attempts to guide them.

- *Bearing ... in love*: the quality we need when others sin against us and unity is seriously endangered.

Look at it from both sides of a disagreement! If both sides exercise all these qualities, will the unity of the church ever be destroyed? These four qualities are like the grievance code that operates in many businesses. If the first stage is not enough, move on to the next, and so on down the list. In the last analysis, *love* will preserve unity and must never be surrendered.

Why all this talk about unity? In verses 4–6 Paul gives the reasons, again looking back to the first half of the letter. In a nutshell, *the church must be one, because God is One*. A divided church cannot be the church of 'the God and Father of our Lord Jesus Christ'.

- Verse 4 focuses on the Spirit who indwells the Body (the church) and moves us to our destiny.

- Verse 5 focuses on Jesus ('one Lord'), whom we confess in faith and baptism.

- Verse 6 focuses on God the Father, who unifies the whole universe, of which the church is a part.

Questions
1. The church of Jesus Christ is divided into many *denominations*. Are these a denial of the unity Paul urges us to have? What should we do about it? (Take care to preserve unity as you discuss this!)
2. 'One faith, one baptism' (verse 5). Another thorny issue! Do you believe that there is 'one faith, one baptism' in the church of Jesus Christ today?
3. There is a clear note of *worship* in verses 4–6, and it may well be that Paul is quoting from a little hymn or creed here. See if you can turn it into a prayer or song.

'Calling'

In verses 1 and 4 Paul talks about the 'calling' we have received. He does not mean, here, the *individual* calling that God has given to each of us, to be a Christian wife, husband, teacher, engineer, or whatever. He means the general 'call' that God has given to all of us, to be joined to Christ. It has more power than just an 'invitation', because it started when he 'chose us in him before the creation of the world' (1:4). It is more like the 'call' that draws the flocks of Canada geese northward from the Gulf of Mexico every spring to breed in the Arctic thousands of kilometres away. They hear the 'call' as the weather warms, and respond to it with all their energy. So each of us *hears God's call* when we first respond to the Good News of Jesus Christ, and then we *have a calling*, which is to pursue the journey that lies ahead of us.

Paul has described the special 'calling' of the church in Ephesians 3:10, though he does not use the word there. It is to show God's wisdom to the 'powers', by displaying *already* the unity which God intends for the whole universe. To 'walk worthy of the call', therefore, is to travel in perfect unity, like those lines of geese carefully keeping their V-formation as they pass overhead.

Paul also writes about 'calling' in, for example, Romans 8:30; 1 Corinthians 1:9; 7:15–24; Galatians 1:6, 15; Colossians 3:15; 1 Thessalonians 4:7; 2 Thessalonians 2:14; 2 Timothy 1:9.

113

Ephesians 4:7–12

Exercising ministry

The *unity* of the church is not undermined by the *diversity* of the gifts Christ has given to us. In fact, his varied gifts are meant to build a unified ministry.

Principle no. 2 in the Constitution of the church of Jesus Christ: it *serves*. And this does not mean that *only certain people serve*, those officially labelled 'Minister'. We are *all* called to service. Paul is emphatic: 'to each one of us grace has been given as Christ apportioned it' (verse 7). Here he uses 'grace' in a special sense, meaning the *special gift of grace which is a spiritual gift or ministry, given for the good of the whole church* (see also Rom. 1:5; 12:6 – and Eph. 3:7–8).

Paul describes such 'spiritual gifts' also in Romans 12:4–8 and 1 Corinthians 12:1–31. There he lists many more gifts than just the five he mentions here in verse 11. In both places (but especially 1 Cor. 12) he makes it clear that these are not gifts *to* each of us, but gifts *through* each of us *to* the whole church. This comes out here in verse 12, where Paul tells us why Christ has given apostles, prophets, evangelists, pastors and teachers to his church: 'to prepare God's people for works of service, so that the body of Christ may be built up' (verse 12). Here the 'works of service' are to be performed by 'God's people', and this is where all the *other* spiritual gifts come in, the ones in the longer lists in Romans 12 and 1 Corinthians 12.

But Ephesians 4:7–12 is different from Romans 12 and 1 Corinthians 12, because here Paul attaches the giving of the gifts to *a Scriptural quotation* (verse 8), which he then uses to say something very profound about the *significance* of the giving of these gifts. The quotation is drawn from Psalm 68:18. We will tackle the details of the quotation below in *Paul's quotation of Psalm 68:18*, for Paul seems to change the meaning of the verse! But, leaving that difficulty on one side, we look at verses 8–10 and ask, What does he teach here about gifts and ministries within the church? These verses are certainly rather puzzling but we can summarize Paul's teaching as follows:

The gifts are a sign of his victorious ascension. Verse 8, using the language of Psalm 68:18, pictures Jesus as a victorious king returning from battle and giving gifts to his subjects to mark his victory. This is what has happened at the ascension of Jesus to God's right hand, says Paul. He 'led captivity captive' (literal translation). Paul the prisoner, sitting under house arrest in Rome, knows that *he is only an apostle because Jesus is victorious over every enemy, and over all the 'powers' which still seem so powerful.* 'Apostles' are the first gift given by the reigning, exalted Lord Jesus (verse 11). So who is the real prisoner? Paul, or his Roman captors who are still following 'the ruler of the kingdom of the air' (2:2)?

He has left defeated enemies behind on earth. Verse 9 has puzzled scholars greatly. Whatever does Paul mean? In this case, the best approach is probably to avoid the details of a difficult debate, and I will simply present the view which seems to me to make sense.

Applying Psalm 68:18 to Jesus, Paul asks, What is *implied* by saying 'he ascended'? His answer is, Jesus must have first *descended*. How else could he then *ascend*? Now Psalm 68 is all about God going into battle against the enemies of his people and defeating them (see below). So it is easy for Paul to apply this to Jesus and to say that he has done the same. At his ascension, he left behind a battle-field littered with the bodies of defeated enemies. Who are these enemies? Not human ones, to be sure, but spiritual, the 'rulers and authorities' whose defeat is announced by the church in which Jews and Gentiles are one (3:10). The phrase 'lower, earthly regions' is vague, and has more than a whiff of Hell about it, as well as including this earth on which we live (see Psalm 63:9, 139:15; 1 Peter 3:19). That is where this ascended Lord has won his victory!

But how does this fit in with the theme of *spiritual gifts in the church?* The answer follows on:

The gifts are part of his strategy for uniting heaven and earth. This comes out in verse 10. What a dramatic idea! The thought is that, through his incarnation, resurrection and ascension, and through the *victory* he has won, Jesus binds together heaven and earth, in fact 'the whole universe' (verse 10). The object of it all is 'so that he might fill all things' (literal translation). So now, exalted and reigning, he gives gifts which serve *to build up his body* (verse 12), and thus to bring closer the day when God will 'bring all things in heaven and earth under one head, even Christ' (1:10).

Remember: he is 'head over everything for the church, which is his body, the fulness of him who fills everything in every way' (1:22–23). Well, the church is *heading towards* being the full Body of Christ in which heaven and earth are united. But we need to *grow* first (4:13). And *that's* why he has given gifts of ministries to his church!

Questions
1. What church is Paul talking about in this passage? The universal church, or each local church? Think of ways in which *both* are built up through the ministries Jesus has given.
2. 'Apostles and prophets' appear earlier, in 2:20 and 3:5. Do you think that there are apostles and prophets alive in the church today? If not, has Jesus withdrawn this gift? How is their ministry still effective?
3. Are you being equipped 'for works of service'? How effective is your church in fulfilling the vision of verse 12? What could these 'works of service' be, for you and your church?

Paul's quotation of Psalm 68:18

Paul certainly causes a puzzle here! But it can be solved.

The problem is that the verse actually says, 'When you ascended on high, you led captives in your train; you received gifts from men'. It pictures God as a victorious general *receiving* gifts, not giving them. Paul has deliberately (apparently) altered the verse so that it talks about *giving* gifts, and therefore fits the idea he wants it to express. To solve this puzzle, we need to look more closely at Psalm 68, and at how others were interpreting it in Paul's day. It is important to turn to Psalm 68 now.

It is a fascinating Psalm! It is very poetic, painting powerful word-pictures to prompt worship, rather like Ephesians. It is about *three things at the same time* and its power and beauty lie in the connection it makes these three things:

- It is about Israel's journey from Egypt to the Promised Land (see especially verses 6–10). But this is only on the surface:

- More importantly, it is about a journey that *God* makes, accompanying his people. He leads them out of Egypt (verse 7), having defeated his enemies, and then journeys with his people, from Sinai to Jerusalem where he ascends 'into his sanctuary' (verse 17). 'His sanctuary' is of course the Temple in Jerusalem, but the Temple there was regarded as an earthly copy of his *heavenly* sanctuary.

- It is also about a procession up the Temple Mount – quite possibly one in which the ark of God is being carried into the Temple. 'Your procession has come into view, O God, the procession of my God and King into the sanctuary!' (verse 24).

So God is entering his Temple. He comes victorious over the enemies who held his people captive. He has travelled and fought with them. He brings his enemies captive behind him (verse 22). The kings of the earth bring him gifts in homage (verse 29, cf. verse 18). Because of his victory, the whole world is called to come and worship him (verses 32–33). 'Proclaim the power of God, whose majesty is over Israel, whose power is in the skies. You are awesome, O God, in your sanctuary; the God of Israel gives power and strength to his people!' (verses 34–35).

Paul simply applies all this to Jesus. In the ascension of Jesus to the *heavenly* Temple, he sees the *supreme* victory of God over his enemies – not over human enemies, the kings of Egypt and Bashan, but over the 'rulers and authorities'. And just as the victorious God gave his 'power and strength' to Israel, so the victorious Christ gives gifts to his church. Paul has altered the quotation in order to bring it into line with the wider message of the Psalm.

Actually, he was not the only one to alter this verse from 'receiving' to 'giving'. The same change had been made in one Jewish tradition, in which the verse was applied (inappropriately) to *Moses going up Mount Sinai*. Moses was the one who 'ascended on high' and then 'gave gifts to men' in the form of the Law which he received on Sinai to give to Israel. Did Paul know of this Jewish tradition? Quite possibly. And so he may have wanted to oppose it, and apply it instead to Jesus. His interpretation of the Psalm is much more appropriate.

This quotation is one of those in which passages applied to *God* in the Old Testament are applied to *Jesus* in the New Testament: see also, for example, Psalm 8:2 in Matthew 21:16, Isaiah 45:23 in Philippians 2:10, and Isaiah 44:6 in Revelation 1:17.

Five orders of ministry?

Are the five ministries listed in 4:11 a blueprint for a fully-equipped church? If a church doesn't have all five, is it inadequate? Some churches pride themselves on having all five 'orders' of ministry functioning today.

This is one of those points over which Christians and churches will disagree, and therefore we must bring into action Paul's plan for unity in disagreement: see 4:2!

● Some feel that *apostleship* is still a living ministry in the church today. Apostles, they say, are those especially gifted and appointed to *plant churches* (see Eph. 2:20) and to be final, authoritative leaders for whole groups of churches. Many others, however, believe that the apostles of the New Testament exercised a bigger ministry than this – in fact, a unique, unrepeatable ministry as those to whom the 'mystery' was revealed (3:5). But they are not dead. They are still present in the church – *through their writings*. That is why we spend so much time and effort producing books about the New Testament (and reading them!).

● *Prophecy* too is a source of disagreement. Some feel that they, too, had a unique ministry alongside the apostles as the channels of revelation to the church. They point to the way in which they are 'bracketed' with the apostles in 1 Corinthians 12:28, and in these three places in Ephesians (2:20, 3:5 and 4:11). But others feel that New Testament prophets were not as 'exalted' as apostles, and that they continue in the church today as channels of 'words' from God.

● There is no disagreement about the other three ministries, evangelists, pastors and teachers. Like apostles and prophets, these three are ministries of *speech*, in different ways: evangelists speak the Gospel to unbelievers, teachers speak it to believers, and pastors speak to guide and lead the church in its evangelism and ministry.

That gives us the clue, I believe, to all these ministries. Why does Paul single them out, and not mention many of the other gifts which he lists in Romans 12 and 1 Corinthians 12? The answer is that *these are the ministries of the Word, on which all other ministries rest*. They are the mouthpiece of Christ who speaks to his church, his body, through them. So they are *foundation* gifts, signalling the real presence of the Lord of the universe in his church.

Ephesians 4:13–16

Developing maturity

Where is it all leading? Paul tells us what the real *reason* for all ministry is: to help the church to 'grow up into Christ'.

Principle no. 3 in the Constitution: growth. Christ *plans* the growth of the church, his body. That is why he has given these gifts of ministry. And there is no doubt about it: the church will grow. It will reach the *maturity* which is Christ's will for it. This is very encouraging! – especially for those of us who belong to small, weak, even shrinking churches.

Actually verse 13 is in the middle of another of Paul's long sentences. It runs from verse 11 to verse 16, and consists of 124 words all focused on this theme of growth empowered by ministry:

- Verses 11–12 and 16 describe *how* the growth of the body takes place.

- Verse 13 describes the *ultimate* aim of the ministries that produce growth: 'the whole measure of the fulness of Christ'.

- Verses 14–15 describe the *immediate* aim of the ministries that produce growth: to make us secure in a confusing and false world, so that we can grow, fed by the truth.

We will look at each of these in turn:

How does the Body grow?   This long sentence begins and ends on this theme. Actually Paul uses the expression 'build up' in verses 12 and 16, which is a strange one to use in connection with a *body*. It is more appropriate for a *building* ... which of course explains why

Paul uses it, because he is carrying it over from the *Temple* picture of the church in 2:20–22 (and in 3:17–19).

The Temple, you remember, is still under construction (2:21–22). But there is something very special about the way this Temple is growing, something which does not actually fit with the 'building' picture. The fact is, *this building is constructing itself*. Such a thing was never heard of among buildings – but it happens all the time with bodies! My 13-year-old son is now as tall as my wife. Help! Soon I shall be begging him for mercy. How did this monster get so big? All we did was shovel food in and wait. It *just happened*.

Because bodies are like that. And so is the church, the Body of Christ. In verse 16 Paul says three things about this growth:

- It is *from the Head, Jesus*. Paul is probably thinking of Jesus as the source of the Body's nourishment (he is the Giver of the ministries).

- It is *'by every supporting ligament'*. The Body forms a harmonious whole – or should. Each part is vital to the growth of the whole.

- It takes place *'as each part does its work'*. No passengers allowed. Baby-sized feet on an adult body? A horrible thought. Each part needs to join in the growth of the whole.

What will maturity be like? My very first duty as a newly appointed pastor was to take the funeral of a 19-year-old boy who had suddenly died of a rare (and hidden) heart condition. His family was devastated. And part of their agony was the loss of *his future*. They would never see him fully grown, mature, married, a father, a businessman ... Parents look forward to their children growing up, and wonder what their *maturity* will be like. They hope that it will make the effort of rearing them worthwhile!

In verse 13 Paul gives us a snapshot of the future maturity of the church. The church will grow 'until we all arrive at the unity of the faith and of the knowledge of the Son of God, at a "mature man", at the measure of the stature of the fulness of Christ' (literal translation). All disunity will be gone, we will know Jesus (the Body's Head) fully and perfectly, and we will have received from him all that he can give to enable us to enjoy perfect union with him, made into a Body fit for this Head!

What does growth mean for us, right now?   In verse 13 Paul is thinking of the church *as a whole*, the church universal, and its ultimate maturity in Christ. In verses 14–15 he applies the same thoughts to the church in *each place*. If the *whole church* is to reach that maturity, then *each church* must grow ... and ministries are provided in each place to enable that to happen. We must 'in all things grow up into him, who is the Head' (verse 15).

The ministry-gifts of Christ will do two things, to enable us to grow:

● They will enable us to avoid error (verse 14). Paul probably is not thinking of a specific error or false teaching in this verse. He has in mind the whole range of wrong ideas with which we might get infected – or rather, blown and tossed around like a cork in a storm. We need stability, security, steadiness, and that's what these gifts will provide.

● They will enable us to 'speak the truth in love' (verse 15). This is the other side of the same coin. How can we avoid being tossed around by wrong ideas? By being so well anchored to the *truth* that nothing will move us. And this is not just truth as head-knowledge. It is truth *lived out* – something we *speak*, expressed 'in love'.

That's how the church grows!

Questions

1. Make a list of 'the marks of a mature church', based on Ephesians 4:1–16. How does your own fellowship match up? What could you (or your group) do to encourage growth?

2. Paul seems to emphasize the role of the *speaking* ministries (verse 11) in leading the church to maturity. Why is this? Are they more important than other kinds of ministry? In what other ways does the growth of the church depend on *speaking*?

3. Do you think that the maturity Paul describes in verse 13 will only be reached in heaven? Or can the church expect to get there on earth? – And is this maturity for each of us individually, or for all of us together?

Christ, the Head of the Body

The thought that Jesus is the 'head' of 'his body', the church, only comes in Ephesians (1:22f; 4:15f; 5:23) and Colossians (1:18).

When Paul writes about the church as 'the body of Christ' in 1 Corinthians 12 (see especially 12:27), he seems to mean 'the body which belongs to Christ', using 'body' in the sense in which we would use it, for instance, to talk about 'the student body'. A group with a single *identity* can be called 'a body' – and the church is a group like that. We have a single identity because we are all 'of Christ'.

But in Ephesians Paul seems to go further. The difference is that here he talks about Jesus as the 'head' of the body. This apparently makes him *part* of the body! In 1 Corinthians 12 there is no hint that Jesus is the 'head' in this way (see 12:16–21). We need to be very careful and ask, Why does Paul make this change in Ephesians, and can Jesus really be *part* of his church?

'Head' and 'Body' are both *metaphors*. That is, they are picture-words used to help us understand. We use metaphors all the time in conversation – for instance, someone might come out of a group Bible study saying, 'Wow! That was dynamite!' A glance into the room confirms that the furniture has not been blown to shreds, so we have to ask ourselves, What points of *comparison* could there be between a Bible study and dynamite? And we might decide that the study was exciting, surprising, life-changing, shocking – any or all of these. Similarly, when Paul uses these metaphors 'head' and 'body', we must decide what they mean when applied to Christ and the church.

In 4:15–16 Paul is looking back to 1:22–23, where he described Jesus as 'head over all things for the church, which is his body, his fulness ...' Here 'head over all things' suggests authority and rule, and that certainly fits the context. But 'for the church, which is his body' suggests a further meaning for 'head'. When we looked at it, I suggested that Paul – reverently but boldly – is thinking of Jesus as *incomplete* without the church, so deeply has he united himself to us. 'Head' and 'body' together express *mutual dependence, intimacy, belonging, and deep union*. So Jesus shares his *rule* (=headship) with the church, to which he is intimately united (=head of the body).

123

One of the things about metaphors is that their meaning can change from place to place. If someone said 'That was dynamite!' after eating a curry, the points of comparison would be quite different! So we cannot assume that 'head' and 'body' express the same thoughts in 4:15–16. Are there differences? Here the context is changed by the idea of *growth*. This is expressed in two ways:

a. the body is to 'grow up into him' (verse 15), and

b. it is joined and held together 'from him' (verse 16).

As we noted above (b) suggests the *nourishment* of the body from the head: Jesus as the giver of the gifts makes his body grow. But what about (a)? Of course bodies don't grow up into their heads. But they do grow into *maturity*, and Paul has already said that the maturity of the church is nothing less than the stature of Christ himself (verse 13). He is the goal of the church's growth. But in this case, when the church has reached that goal, it will not just be *like* him, it will be *one with* him. Then we will have reached 'the oneness of the faith' and we will 'know' him fully (verse 13).

The point is, our *union* with him is not complete yet. We do not yet know him fully. The Temple is still under construction! We need to 'grow up into him'. He, as our 'head', supplies the nourishment for the growth, and we (the church) grow ever closer to him until finally we reach his 'fulness' (4:13).

So as well as *intimacy* and *union*, calling Jesus 'head' in 4:15 seems to express the thoughts of *supply* (nourishment) and *goal* (*complete union*, 'fulness').

8

THE CHURCH OF CHRIST IN EVERY-DAY LIFE

Ephesians 4:17 – 5:21

Setting the scene

Paul has given us the *Constitution* of the church. Now he gives us the *practice* of the church. What does it actually mean in practice, to belong to this 'body of Christ' which is growing up into him? This teaching, addressed to the first-century church, has powerful things to say to the church of the twenty-first century.

This long section of the letter falls into five sections, as a glance at the contents page of this book will show. We can look ahead over the ground that Paul covers:

- In 4:17–24 he describes *the new Christian mind*. Our *thinking* must be different.

- In 4:25–32 he describes *the new Christian speech*. Our *talking* must be different.

- In 5:1–6 he describes *the new Christian motivation*. Our *impulses* must be different.

- In 5:7–14 he describes *the new Christian lifestyle*. Our *fellowship* must be different.

- In 5:15–21 he describes *the new Christian worship*. Our *time* must be different.

In each section, Paul emphasizes our *unity with each other* as members of the Body of Christ. This unity must be protected and strengthened by the way we think, speak, feel, behave and worship. What a challenge!

Ephesians 4:17–24

Thinking Christianly

Before we became Christians, our chief problem was the *corruption of our minds*. Now that we are Christians, our chief need is the *restoration of our minds*.

This section falls into two paragraphs, following a pattern which we see repeated frequently in Ephesians:

- Verses 17–19, the *negative* picture: futility, darkness, ignorance and insensitivity.

- Verses 20–24, the *positive* picture: truth, teaching, and renewal.

This emphasis on *thinking* and on the *mind*, both negative and positive, is typical of Paul. See for instance Romans 8:5–8; 12:1–2; 1 Corinthians 14:6–19; Philippians 4:8; Colossians 3:1–2. And he does not just deal with the mind in one paragraph and then leave it behind. It is basic to all the instructions which follow. And it follows on from 4:1–16, for the chief ministries which Jesus has given are *speaking* ministries, and therefore address our *minds*. We need to hear, and to be totally changed by what we hear!

Don't live like that! (verses 17–19). 'I insist on it in the Lord', Paul says, as he tells the Ephesians that they must leave their old, pagan, pre-Christian ways of thinking behind. Such 'Gentile' minds are marked by four things:

- They are 'futile' (verse 17). This means that their minds do not do what they are supposed to, like wheels that refuse to turn. Minds are supposed to learn and to understand the *truth*, but these do not.

- They are 'darkened in understanding ... ignorant' (verse 18).
  Says Paul, you will turn in vain to non-Christians to learn the
  truth. From non-Christian teachers, all you will get is 'ignorance'. In *Truth in other religions?* (p. 131) we will think further
  about this very powerful claim.

- They are 'separated from the life of God' (verse 18). Minds
  should think in harmony with God's mind, touched by his Spirit. But non-Christian minds cannot.

- And finally they are *hard and insensitive* (verses 18–19). Paul is
  thinking of the things associated with pagan religion, where sexual immorality and child abuse were not just permitted but
  prized.

Live out the new mind instead! (verses 20–24).   'You did not learn
Christ that way', Paul says (verse 20, literal translation), referring to
the practices of pagan life and religion just mentioned. Christ can
never be found by that route. How did they 'learn Christ', then?
Verses 21–24 spell out the route by which they are getting to know
him. Remember, 'the knowledge of the Son of God' is one of the
goals towards which the church is heading (4:13). When we are
mature, then we will know him. So how do we become mature?
Again, Paul lists four things:

- *Teaching* (verse 21). The Christians to whom Paul is writing have
  already received the essential teaching they need. They have
  learned the particular 'truth that is in Jesus'. What is this teaching?

- *Putting off the old self* (verse 22). The leopard can never change
  his spots, they say. But this is not true for Christians. You know
  how to do it! says Paul. Through the teaching they have
  received, they have learned *that they must,* and also *how they can.*
  In verse 22 Paul looks back to 2:1–3 and the corruption of nature
  from which the Ephesians have been delivered. Once they could
  do nothing about the pressure of their own desires. They were
  enslaved – to money, sex, power. But now they have learned
  how to be free, how to 'put off the old self', or (literally) 'the old
  person'.

- *Being renewed in mind* (verse 23). This is the second of the three things Paul says they have been taught in verses 22–24. A literal translation would be, 'you were taught ... how to go on being made new in the spirit of your mind'. Paul is thinking not of a *moment*, but of a *process* of renewal, which they have been taught to keep going. The motor must not be allowed to stall. They must go on re-shaping their thinking until it is *Christian* through and through.

- *Putting on the new self* (verse 24). They have also learned how to 'put on the new self, created to be like God in true righteousness and holiness'. Here Paul is thinking back to 2:15, where he spoke of the 'one new person' which Christ has created in himself, bringing together Jews and Gentiles into a whole new body, the church. A new creation, a new 'person', a new type of being ... To 'put' on this new person' means *actually to become, in practice, what God intends this new human being to be like*. He intends us to be like himself – marked by *righteousness* and *holiness*.

The NIV has 'true righteousness and holiness', but I think that the paraphrase above is better. This righteousness and holiness *come from the truth*. If the shop of our mind is stocked with truth, then *righteousness* and *holiness* will be displayed in the window.

Questions
1. Paul reminds the Ephesians that they 'were taught' how to 'put off ... be renewed ... put on', but he doesn't actually say what this teaching was. *How can we* get rid of 'the old self' and put on the new? Think *practically*.
2. Why do you think that Paul lays such emphasis on the *mind* and *thinking* here? Do you think that our minds can ever be an *obstacle*, stopping us from growing in Christ?
3. Think about Paul's analysis of Gentile society in verses 17–19. Is the society in which you live like this? What's the best strategy for Christian outreach, to a society where minds are corrupt and cannot see the truth?

Truth in other religions?

'Futile minds ... darkened understanding ... ignorance ... insensitivity' – that is Paul's description of Gentile society in verses 17–19. Let's reflect for a moment. The society he is describing produced some of the greatest philosophers and writers the world has ever known – Socrates, Plato, Aristotle and many others. These Greek thinkers deeply influenced not only western society, but also *many Christian theologians*. For instance, Saint Augustine (one of the greatest of all theologians) tells us in his *Confessions* (his spiritual autobiography) that he found nearly the whole truth in Greek philosophy: the only part he did not discover there was that Truth had become *flesh* in Jesus Christ.

But here in Ephesians Paul seems to write off all this Gentile learning as 'futile ... ignorance!' Was Augustine wrong to value it so highly? This question is important for us, because we face the same issue today. Is there truth outside Christianity, in other religions and philosophies?

Opinions vary greatly among Christians today. Some would be happy to say that *Christianity is only one way among many to God*, one truth among many truths. At the opposite end of the spectrum others would write all other religions off as 'futile ... ignorance!' – and this second group seems, at first sight, to be true to Paul.

But let's not be too hasty. In Titus 1:12–13 Paul quotes approvingly from a non-Christian Greek poet called Epimenides. 'This testimony is true!' he says, and calls Epimenides 'a prophet'. Even more striking, in his sermon in Athens recorded by Luke in Acts 17:22–31, he quotes another line from the same Epimenides, and then adds a quotation from a hymn to the Greek god Zeus, written by a Stoic poet called Aratus: 'We are his offspring'. Yes, says Paul to the crowd of non-Christians in front of him, we are indeed his offspring – you and I together (Acts 17:28–29). And he mentions the altar 'to an unknown god', which shows a true awareness of a greatness and a mystery not yet grasped (Acts 17:23).

It seems as though Paul was ready to recognize *truth* in other religions, but not of course the *whole truth*. He uses the insight of Aratus to say, 'So we ought not to make idols and worship them, and now God calls all mankind to repent because he is to judge the world through Jesus' (Acts 17:29–31, literal translation). Aratus has only gone so far, and needs to go much further.

But why then does Paul talk so blackly about darkness and ignorance in Ephesians 4:17–19? There are probably two reasons:

1. In a dark room, the light from a candle seems quite bright. But when the sunlight streams in, the candlelight disappears completely. So, in view of what we *can* know of God in Christ, the very little that Aratus or Plato *did* know about him is *ignorance* by *comparison*. In Romans 1:19–21 Paul says that people generally 'know God' just through looking at his creation. But all they know is 'his eternal power and divine nature' – nothing more. Nothing about his justice, or his love, or his Son.

   I believe that we can take the same view of the great religions and 'isms' of the world. There is undoubtedly truth in them. But what pale truth, compared with what he has revealed in Christ (Eph. 1:9–10, 3:2–6)!

2. In any case, Paul is not thinking just of the great philosophies in Ephesians 4:17–19. He is thinking mainly of *pagan religion*. He had seen it all on the streets of Ephesus when he lived there: the cult prostitutes associated with the temples and shrines, the public display of immorality, the greed fed by idolatry, the open sexual exploitation of children, especially of boys, by the lazy rich, the soothsayers and magicians making money out of people's lust or fear, the demonic oppression – and all this in the name of 'devotion' to a god or goddess. There was little truth of any kind to be seen in *that*. It was just a horrible *un*truth, a cruel mess of 'deceitful desires' (4:22). He was ready to call ignorance by its proper name – and so should we.

Ephesians 4:25–32

Speaking truthfully

A renewed *mind* leads to transformed *speech*. Paul puts his finger on some difficult but vital areas where Christians must be *different*.

What is the most important thing we can do for each other, as Christians? Care for each other? Pray? Give encouragement? Be ready to *die* for each other if necessary? Paul does not hesitate: ahead of all these, we must *tell each other the truth*.

Out of the renewed mind comes new speech. This whole paragraph focuses on speech, in different ways:

- Lying (verse 25)

- Anger (verses 26–27)

- Stealing (verse 28: this too relates to speech, as we shall see)

- Criticism (verse 29).

The paragraph ends with a beautiful summary of what *motivates* pure speech (verses 30–32): the presence of the Holy Spirit, and the grace of God in Christ.

Paul handles each of the four topics in verses 25–29 in the same way. (1) A *negative* command (don't!) is followed by (2) a *positive* command (do!), followed in turn by (3) a *reason* to support what Paul says. We will see how this works out as we look at each:

- *Lying* (verse 25). Put off all this falsehood (negative)! Speak truthfully to your neighbour (positive)! For we are all members of one body (reason)! If we belong to the one body of Christ, then *there must be truth between us*. We must 'speak the truth in love' (4:15). Truth is the blood-supply of the body of Christ.

● *Anger* (verses 26–27). In your anger do not sin (negative)! Don't let the sun set on your anger (negative, but positive in effect: be reconciled quickly!). Don't give the devil a foothold (reason)! Anger *may* be right, but even when right it is *dangerous*, because it might lead to disunity in the one body (see 4:2–3). Sort it out quickly – otherwise the devil has won.

● *Stealing* (verse 28). Don't steal (negative)! Do good work with your hands (positive)! – so that you will have something to give away (reason). Stealing is related to speech because it relies on an *absence* of speech, it is secretive, it conceals the truth, goes behind someone's back. It deals in falsehood and deception. And here's something remarkable. What's the whole point of working and earning? In the body of Christ, it is *not* for yourself. We work and earn *so that we will have something to give away*. Revolutionary!

● *Criticism* (verse 29). No horrible talk (negative)! Only what is helpful for others (positive)! – so that it may bring *grace* to those who hear (reason). This is just as remarkable as the last verse. What's the whole point of *speaking*? In the body of Christ, again, it is not for yourself. The purpose of speaking is not *self-expression*, but giving 'grace' to others, building them up according to their need. Yes, revolutionary!

Verses 30–32 round the whole paragraph off by bringing our relationship to God into the picture. Paul has given reasons with each instruction, but now he gives the final, basic reason for *making pure speech an absolute priority in our relationships with each other*. As so often in Ephesians, he draws each person of the Trinity into it, the Holy Spirit in verse 30, and the Father and the Son in verse 32.

'Do not grieve the Holy Spirit of God, with whom you were sealed for the day of redemption!' (verse 30). The point is, the Holy Spirit is present in us, and in the church, because it is through him that we are being prepared for final 'redemption': and *he is hurt by rotten speech between us*. What kind of speech hurts him? Paul tells us in verse 31. Here he lists five kinds of speech which 'grieve' the

Holy Spirit. They gradually get worse and worse:

● Bitterness (complaining, moaning)

● Rage (a sudden loss of temper)

● Anger (that loss of temper continues, becomes an *attitude*)

● Brawling (anger breaks out in open hostility and shouting)

● Slander (the result of it all – character-assassination, perhaps behind people's backs).

If all this happens, no wonder the Spirit is grieved. The last word, 'slander', is actually the word 'blasphemy', which is often used of *evil talk against God*. Perhaps Paul uses this word on purpose, because to slander our fellow-Christians is to abuse the Holy Spirit who is preparing them for 'redemption'. Away with all this! says Paul. Instead ...

Instead (verse 32), they must treat each other as God has treated them, in Christ. This means *kindness, compassion*, and *forgiveness*. Words that express these things will match the words of blessing that God has spoken to us, in Christ.

Questions

1. Take some time to reflect very carefully, and to pray, about the way you usually speak *to*, and *about*, fellow-Christians. What are your motives? Just self-expression? Or building them up?

2. In the early church they believed and acted upon verse 28: see Acts 2:44–45, 4:32. The practice of having a common fund continued long after New Testament times. In the light of this, what do you think about the way the finances of your church or denomination are operated?

3. Under what circumstances may a Christian be angry? (Note: in verse 26 Paul is quoting Psalm 4:4.)

Ephesians 5:1–6

Loving sacrificially

Paul contrasts two kinds of love: Christian love, and pagan love. He knows that his readers could be deceived into confusing them with each other. We could be, too.

 Quite a few writers think that Ephesians 5:1–2 really belongs with chapter 4, finishing it off with a beautiful description of the love of Christ which we should imitate. And it certainly does follow on from 4:32. Paul deliberately balances the sentences:

- 4:32: forgive one another, *as God forgave you* ...

- 5:2: walk in love, *as Christ loved you* ...

And in between these he tells us to 'be imitators of God'. Typical of Paul: he tells us to imitate *God*, and then shows us the example of *Christ*.

So there is no break between 4:32 and 5:1. But the theme of *love* becomes more prominent in 5:1–2, and this leads in to what follows. For in 5:3–6 Paul contrasts the *love of Christ* with the *pretended, false love* offered by pagan religion (both then and now). Pagan religion could look very attractive (as it does now): but Paul wants to expose it for what it really is, and to remind his readers of where *true love* is seen and found.

Chapter 5:1–2 actually lays the foundation for the rest of the chapter, and underlies all that Paul says. He comes back to the theme of love in 5:25–53.

True love – only in Jesus (5:1–2)   'Live a life of love' (verse 2, NIV) is literally 'walk in love'. This translation appears in some older

Bibles, for instance the *Revised Standard Version*. 'Walk in love' is actually a better translation, for it includes the thought that *love is something we receive*, as well as something we give or express. Love is to be the air we breathe – we breathe it *in*, and we breathe it *out*.

We are 'dearly loved children' (verse 1) – *of God*. He is the Father who loves us. But the love in which we must walk is the love *of Christ* (verse 2). When Jesus showed his love for us by dying for us, he was showing us the love *of God himself*. And that love we must imitate, in our relationships with one another.

It is a love of total self-sacrifice. Jesus gave himself *for* us, *to* God, *as* a sacrifice. And to 'walk in' this love means first to receive the benefit of it, to bask in its blessings, and then to express the same kind of love ourselves. We too will give ourselves *for* others *to* God – a love that looks in two directions at the same time. God is the *object* of our love, and others the *purpose* of our love. That's how it was for Jesus!

Paul uses Old Testament language in describing Jesus' sacrifice. The animal sacrifices commanded in the Old Testament are some-times called 'an aroma pleasing to the LORD' (Lev. 2:9 – see also Exod. 29:18). Now the animal sacrifices have been replaced by the sacrifice of Jesus. And also by the sacrifice of Jesus' followers. Writ-ing to the Philippians, Paul thanks them for their love expressed in their gifts to him, which were 'a fragrant offering, an acceptable sacrifice, pleasing to God' (Phil. 4:18).

False love – in the world around (5:3–6)   Love expressed by *self-sacrifice* was almost unheard-of in the ancient world. There were occasional examples – for instance, slaves sacrificing themselves for their masters, or acts of great heroism in battle. But even here the mentality was 'death or glory!' This *total* self-sacrifice of Christ, with no thought of self at all, would have seemed very odd to the man or woman on the street in Ephesus. We think of 'humility' as something *good* – Paul tells us to have it in Ephesians 4:2. But in pagan Greek thinking humility was *despised*. The truly good person is the *winner*, the one who is able to take control of his life, be confi-dent, not be defeated by circumstances or by others. Frank Sinatra would have been a sell-out in ancient Ephesus: 'I did it my way!!'

So what was love? Basically, it was *desire*. The good, successful person is the one who manages to fulfil all his or her desires.

This is what forms the connection between 5:1–2, and 5:3–6. If love is *desire*, then the flood-gates open and in rushes ... well, in a word, *paganism*. Paul describes it graphically. Fornication, impurity, greed, obscenity, foolish talk, idolatry ... The mention of idolatry in verse 5 helps us to understand, because all these things were associated with the pagan temples in Ephesus. Pagan religion meant *getting*, not *giving*: the whole point was, can I persuade this god/goddess to give me what I want – money, sex, power, success? Perhaps I can get it by making an offering, or paying some money and 'worshipping' with a temple prostitute.

Christians could be tempted by this. It was the environment in which they had grown up. It meant a complete change of mind-set, a revolution in their outlook, to take on board the Christian understanding of love as *self-sacrifice*, following the example of Jesus. And you must! says Paul. 'No immoral, impure or greedy person – that is, no *idolater* – has any inheritance in the Kingdom of Christ and of God. Let no-one deceive you with empty words!' (verses 5–6).

Questions

1. How do you think your society compares with ancient Greek society? How can we help each other to resist the pressures of a society oriented around *desire* and *self-fulfilment*?

2. Paul tells the Ephesians that 'sexual immorality, all impurity and greed should not be named among you, as is proper and right for God's holy people' (verse 3 – literal translation: see also verse 12). What does he mean, and how should we obey this practically?

3. How are you, and your church, managing so far as *walking in love* is concerned? Is God prompting you to take any particular steps along that path?

Ephesians 5:7–14

Shining attractively

How are we to live in a society which follows completely different values from us? Paul explains. The key idea: *separation* but not *seclusion*.

There is no real break at verse 7, but Paul begins that verse with a 'therefore!' which suggests that he is drawing conclusions from what he has just said. And when we look at verses 7–14, we can see that he has moved on from our *attitude* towards pagan society around us, to think about our *action* towards it. What should we actually *do*, how should we actually *live*, surrounded by a society which lives by completely different values? This is the question which Paul tackles as far as the next 'therefore' in verse 15.

His answer has two parts to it:

Separation (verses 7–11)   'Do not be partners with them!' he begins (verse 7). 'Partners' is the same word as the one he used in 3:5 when he talked about how, through the Gospel, Gentile Christians have been made 'sharers together' with Jewish believers in the promises that previously had just belonged to Israel. They have been made members of this new body, 'partners' in the 'new person' which God has created in Christ. So how can they possibly be 'partners' with the pagan world? They must live an entirely separate life. This is because of *four great differences between them and the world around*:

● They have a different *nature* (verse 8). They are as different from the pagan world as light is from darkness. The two cannot mix! They have been *saved from it* ('once you were ...') and made completely new.

139

- They have a different *lifestyle* (verse 9). From their new nature (light) flows a new life – or rather, grows a new fruit: 'all goodness, righteousness and truth'. The little word 'all' makes the point. In this lifestyle, there must be *nothing but* goodness, righteousness and truth.

- They have a different *Lord* (verse 10). Their lives must be devoted to finding out what is pleasing to him – and then, of course, to doing it. *He* directs them, not the world around.

- They have a different *fellowship* (verse 11). 'Have nothing to do with' is literally 'do not have fellowship with'. Paul returns to the point he made in verse 7. How can they have 'fellowship' with the evil practices that go on around them? They cannot! They must be *separate*.

But separation does not mean seclusion. Paul could, of course, have told them to withdraw to a distant mountain-top and wait for 'the day of redemption' (4:30). But he does not.

Exposure (verses 11–14)   They must not withdraw. They must stay in Ephesus, and 'expose' the works of darkness around them (verses 11, 13). What does this mean? It is important to say what it does *not* mean. It doesn't mean that they must start a public campaign against the abuses in society, 'exposing' them in the way that political corruption might be 'exposed' by a newspaper. No – Paul reminds them that they must not even *mention* the dreadful things that happen around them (verse 12). He is not thinking of public 'exposure' in that sense. What, then?

This exposure takes place as the light shines (verse 13), and *they are the light, in themselves* (verse 8). *Just by being themselves* they shine a searchlight into the darkness around. They do not need to say anything at all. And in verses 13–14 Paul explains what effect this can have:

- 'Everything exposed by the light becomes illumined' (verse 13: NIV 'visible'): things *shone upon* absorb the light that shines on them. People will begin literally to 'see things in a new light', perhaps begin to change ...

● 'For everything that is illumined *is* light' (verse 14, literal translation): those *shone upon* by the light of the church's new lifestyle
can *become* light themselves, they can join the company of those
who 'are light in the Lord' (verse 8).

To rub these thoughts home, Paul quotes from a little hymn in
verse 14. This is not a quotation from the Old Testament. It is a
piece of early Christian poetry – one of the 'hymns and spiritual
songs' he mentions in 5:19. It could have been especially associated
with *baptism*, perhaps sung just before new believers were baptized. At any rate, this hymn is an *evangelistic appeal to the world
around*. Come and let the light of Christ shine on you! His light
gives new life to the dead. Come and be 'light in the Lord' with us!

Questions
1. What do you think Paul has in mind when he talks of the church
   'finding out what is pleasing to the Lord' (verse 10)? How can
   churches do this?
2. Why does Paul *not* tell the Ephesian Christians (for instance) to
   campaign against child prostitution in the temples of Ephesus? Do
   you think that Christians should ever undertake public or political
   campaigns of that kind?
3. What does this passage have to teach us about evangelism? What
   lessons do you think your church could particularly learn from Paul
   here?

Paul, Artemis and the Gospel

It would be helpful here to glance at the evidence
of Acts about Paul's attitude to the pagan religions
in Ephesus, and his approach to evangelism there.
We read that he set himself up in a lecture-hall
in the middle of town, where he held daily 'discussions' with any
who came in (Acts 19:9). Presumably both Christians and unbelievers were there. Then in the evenings he pastored and taught the
church, both in larger groups and going from house to house (Acts
20:20). He clearly taught with great passion: for three years, he
says, 'I never stopped encouraging and warning each of you, day
and night, with tears!' (Acts 20:31).

From his words to the Ephesian elders in Acts 20:18–35, it is clear that he made *building up the church* the focus of his ministry, and he encourages them to do the same. Yet even though this was his focus, *the church grew so rapidly that, at the end of the three years, the cult of Artemis was seriously threatened* (or at least the livelihood of those who made images of her: see Acts 19:25–27).

What did he do about the paganism around him? Very little, it seems. When the city clerk stood up to try to calm the riot in the theatre, he was able to say, 'You have brought these men here, though they have neither robbed temples nor blasphemed our goddess' (Acts 19:37). Even Demetrius, the enraged silversmith, could only say 'He says that man-made gods are no gods at all' (Acts 19:26) – but many other Jews and Greeks were saying that as well, not just Christians. Paul was clearly well-known and liked, not only by the city clerk, but also by other 'officials of the province, friends of Paul' who were concerned about his safety (Acts 19:31).

Paul's ministry was consistently a positive one: 'I have declared to both Jews and to Greeks that they must turn to God in repentance and have faith in our Lord Jesus ... I have not hesitated to proclaim to you the whole will of God! Keep watch over yourselves and all the flock of which the Holy Spirit has made you overseers' (Acts 20:21, 27–28).

Ephesians 5:15-21

Worshipping wisely

The life of the church needs to be focused around its worship, the vital centre where it grows in the Spirit and in wisdom and understanding.

Paul begins to draw this long section (4:17 – 5:21) on *the Church in every-day life* to a close. His instructions in verses 15–17 are more general, the kind we expect in a summary and conclusion. But there is one vital topic he has not yet touched on – one which takes him back full circle to the picture of the church in 4:11–16: *worship*.

What is this church? It is not just another collection of religious people who follow yet another god. The church *lives in vital union* with Jesus, our ascended Lord, who has showered his gifts on us. Those ministry gifts are on 24-hour call. We need to be there for each other at *all* times. And whenever 'works of service' are performed (4:12), it is because the church is growing up into Christ, according to his plan, and by the power of his Spirit.

But there is a special focus of this *union with Jesus*: that is, when we meet to worship and we can 'go on being filled with the Spirit' (5:18) and take onto our lips the words of *thanksgiving* which are so vital for us.

Paul has just reminded his readers of their worship, by quoting the little hymn in verse 14. So it's not surprising that he deals with this theme directly in verses 18–21. What does he teach, then, in this rounding-off passage? He focuses on the idea of *time*, mentioned in verses 16 and 20:

Buy up all your time for the Lord (verses 15–17)! He knows that the Ephesians need *wisdom* for their daily lives. So he encourages them to 'understand what the Lord's will is' (verse 17). How can they do this? Of course Paul has in mind all those teaching ministries (4:11), which are there to enable the church to hear and understand the Lord's will for our lives. Each of us needs to work hard for *understanding*, so that we truly grasp *for ourselves* what the will of Jesus is for us ('The Lord' = Jesus).

If we can understand his will, then we will not be 'foolish' (verse 17), we will live *wisely* (verse 15), and we will be able to 'redeem the time' (16). This expression in verse 16 is a little puzzling and the NIV has translated it 'making the most of every opportunity'. But it probably means more than this. 'The days are evil', says Paul: the 'ruler of the kingdom of the air' is in charge (2:2), the world around us is corrupt, we live in a world under enemy occupation by the powers of evil. But we can 'redeem' our bit of world history, the days of time available to us – that is, we can buy them up, and rescue them from the clutches of evil, by living them wisely, in obedience to the will of the Lord Jesus who will one day sum up *all* time and history in himself (1:10)! What a challenge – and opportunity.

Let your worship touch all your time (verses 18–21)! Wisdom and understanding are gained through Christ's teaching ministries. But when do they operate? Chiefly when the church gathers for worship. So it is not surprising that Paul turns specifically to this. What he writes about the church at worship is so inspiring. He says five things:

- *It must be different* (verse 18). Why does he mention drunkenness here? The answer almost certainly is because it was such a regular feature of worship in many pagan temples and cults. Alcohol and other drugs would be used to create states of ecstasy and visionary experiences. No, says Paul, not that way. You need to *go on being filled* by the Spirit of God – a continuous process, progressively being filled more and more as we 'grow up into Christ'. Christian worship must be different from that of all other religions!

- *It must be corporate* (verse 19a). The early Christians obviously used many songs known to all the members, which they sang together. (See '*Psalms, hymns and spiritual songs*' below for a few details.) But there is something strange about Paul's instruction here: he does not say, 'Speak *to God* ...', but 'Speak *to one another* ...' They sing *for each other*, to encourage each other by being there together and singing the same words.

● *It must be joyful* (verse 19b). Singing and music are to take place, first and foremost *in the heart* and not in the throat!

● *It must be continued* (verse 20). '*Always* giving thanks ...', Paul says. It is very striking how, throughout this section, he will not let worship be a 'compartment' in our lives, separated from the rest of our time. Thanksgiving must be a little song in our hearts throughout the week. I am convinced that we should translate 'for everything' as 'for everyone' in this verse (it's an equally possible translation).

● *It must be non-hierarchical* (verse 21). This verse just carries on the same sentence from verse 20. There is no break: '... submitting to one another in the fear of Christ'. This is remarkable! We might have expected those with the great ministry-gifts of 4:11 to be somehow 'over' the rest of the church. But no. The whole church, all members, are to worship in a state of *mutual submission*, that is, all are to be equally ready to receive from each other. This is because *all* have a ministry to contribute (1 Cor. 12:7). So even Paul the apostle looks forward to *receiving* as well as giving (see Rom. 1:11–12).

Questions

1. Churches today differ so much in their *styles* of worship: some use set forms of prayer, others don't; some are 'charismatic', others not; some set certain individuals apart to lead, others do not. Do you think that Paul's teaching here favours one style, or all styles?

2. Paul is obviously describing the ideal here. What particular things do you think your church needs to learn? In what ways could you (gently!) encourage the church to grow in worship?

3. How can we 'redeem' all our time, when most of the week is spent busy at work or doing things not directly concerned with the Lord?

'Psalms, hymns and spiritual songs'

What are these? What did the first Christians actually sing in their worship, and what can we learn from them?

The short answer is that we do not know for sure! The obvious suggestion that 'psalms' means the book of Psalms in the Old Testament, and 'hymns and spiritual songs' were *new, Christian compositions* seems not, in fact, likely. All three words are used to describe the Psalms in the Old Testament. It looks as though Christians may well have sung Old Testament Psalms in their worship, because some of them are quoted at length in the New Testament: see for instance 1 Peter 3:10–12; Hebrews 3:7–11; Romans 11:9–10.

But this evidence is not conclusive, because these Psalms may be quoted just as Old Testament Scriptures, and not as hymns currently sung!

It is clear, however, that the first Christians did indeed write many new praise-songs. The Roman writer Pliny actually refers to Christians (some fifty years after the time of Ephesians) getting together daily at dawn to 'recite to one another in turns a hymn to Christ as to God'. And little pieces of these songs have been preserved in the New Testament. We just met one in Ephesians 5:14. Another appears for sure in 1 Timothy 3:16. And it is highly likely that Philippians 2:6–11 and Colossians 1:15–20 are further examples. In addition scholars have *suspected* the presence of praise-songs in (for instance) Romans 1:3–4 and 3:24–26; Ephesians 2:14–16 and 4:5–6; 1 Peter 2:21–25; Hebrews 1:1–4; and of course there are many songs in the book of Revelation which could well be reflections of the worship of the early church (certainly *after* the book was written, if not *before!*).

It seems unlikely, too, that 'spiritual songs' means 'songs sung in the Spirit' – that is, singing in tongues or under direct inspiration of the Spirit. At any rate, songs *in tongues* would not fit with Paul's emphasis here on *speaking to one another* (see what he says about the *private* nature of tongues in 1 Cor. 14:2–12). A 'spiritual song' could certainly be one given by the Spirit, but in 1 Corinthians 14:26 Paul pictures people *coming to the worship* with a 'hymn' to share – presumably one written down at home, which is now taught to the whole church.

SPECIAL
RELATIONSHIPS
Ephesians 5:22 – 6:9

Setting the scene

Paul moves on to a new topic now, as all the translations show us by printing a paragraph-break here, usually after verse 21. 'Wives and Husbands', the NIV tells us, is the new topic. And 'Wives and Husbands' are followed by other family relationships – 'Children and Parents' (6:1–4), and 'Slaves and Masters' (6:5–9). Here Paul employs what writers have called a 'Household Code': a section of teaching on the various relationships within family life (see also Col. 3:18 – 4:1; 1 Pet. 2:18 – 3:7).

What the translations don't tell us is that Paul himself doesn't even have a *sentence*-break here, let alone a new paragraph! In fact, verses 18–23 are all one sentence in Paul's Greek, of 74 words. The fact that he doesn't start a new sentence when he moves on to this new topic shows that, for him, *it is very closely related to what he has just been saying*.

Why? What is the connection between 'Wives and Husbands' and what he has just written about worship? Actually, we should probably ask, what is the connection between *all* the family relationships he now tackles (5:22 – 6:9), and *all* the teaching about the church and its life in 4:1 – 5:21?

The experts give different answers, but the best suggestion seems to be this: Paul realizes that people will be bothered by the question, How does *the family* fit in with all this? Paul has painted such a glowing picture of the church, with us all *belonging to each other*, and finding our reason for existence in serving one another. But don't we also belong to our families? How does commitment to *marriage*, and to *children*, and to *employment*, fit into this all-absorbing commitment to the Body of Christ?

Many Christians today feel this tension sharply. Demanding jobs and a busy family life hardly seem to leave any time for involvement in the ministry of the church. And yet we are taught that what we do in the church and for the Lord is *far more important* than anything else we do. Our jobs are essential – so time-space has to be made at the expense of family life. For many active in their local church, especially in leadership, an evening at home with husband or wife is a rarity. And for their children, Mum's and Dad's typical movement is not *towards* them, to share their time and concerns, but *away from them*, out through the front door to share the time and concerns of others.

And Paul seems to encourage this! He himself had turned his back on family life, and in 1 Corinthians 7:32–34 he encourages others to do so, also: 'I would like you to be free from concern! An unmarried man is concerned about the Lord's affairs – how he can please the Lord. But a married man is concerned about the affairs of this world – how he can please his wife – and his interests are divided.' He says that marriage is all right: 'If you do marry, you have not sinned!' (1 Cor. 7:28). But at the same time he says, 'I wish that all men were as I am' – that is, unmarried (7:7). He seems to teach that marriage, and family life, is a *distraction* from what is really important, serving the Lord in the church.

Is that really the whole picture? This is exactly the issue he tackles in this next section of Ephesians on 'Special Relationships'. In *Families: God's second best?* following 6:5–9 (p. 171), we will come back to this question.

Ephesians 5:22–24

Specially for her

Paul begins his description of *the practice of Christian marriage* with some words for the wife. Submit to your husband, he says, as the Church submits to Christ, its Head.

Some Christians are uncomfortable about Paul's teaching here. Telling wives to 'submit' to their husbands goes against the spirit of the age, particularly in western cultures and churches, where a mood of equality between the sexes prevails. Other Christians feel happier with Paul, and argue that we must resist the spirit of the age and aim for the ideal, in which the husband is to be the 'head', the senior partner, and the wife should 'submit', being willing to let her husband take final responsibility.

It is very important to be aware of the cultural background in Paul's day (see *Marriage and family life in New Testament times* below for a brief sketch). In a word, first century societies were thoroughly 'patriarchal', that is, the man was definitely regarded as the 'head' or 'monarch' in his household, responsible for ruling not only over his wife but over the children and over any slaves or other dependents who might be part of it. He was in sole charge. This pattern was the cultural 'norm', not only in Greek or Gentile societies, but also in Jewish. The very words that Paul uses here, 'head' for the husband and 'submit' for the wife, are used by other writers to describe this pattern.

So at first sight it seems clear: by using the same words, Paul teaches the same system, and expects the husband to be in charge, and the wife to obey.

But is this the right conclusion? It depends on what we make of the little word 'as', which appears in each verse here. Paul insists that this 'head/submit' pattern must be worked out, not 'as' in society around, but 'as' in the relationship between Christ and the church. The words may be the same, but the *model* is completely different. As Christ is the head of the church, so the husband is the head of his wife (verse 23), and *as* the church submits to Christ, so the wife must submit to her husband (verse 24).

This puts us on the spot. It is like one of those crossword clues which say 'Reverse of 3 down', so that we cannot solve it until we have worked out the other clue. Here, Paul makes the teaching about marriage totally dependent on what he has written earlier about Christ as the 'head' of the church. So we have to work that out first, and then we will understand what he is saying here.

So it is vital not to take Paul's teaching out of its context in Ephesians. He calls Jesus 'head' in relation to the church in 1:22–23, and in 4:15–16. It would be a good idea now to review those passages, and perhaps to read again what I wrote about them, in particular *Christ, the Head of the Body* (see pp. 123–24). Then come back to this passage and ask what the metaphor 'head' means, when applied to the husband who models his 'headship' on that of Jesus. What do you think?

In *One way of handling 'Headship'* (p. 160) I have made some suggestions about this.

Questions

1. Remembering that verses 18–23 are all one sentence, how do you think verses 22–24 are affected by verse 21, 'submit to one another out of reverence for Christ' (literally, 'in the fear of Christ')?

2. What level of priority do you think *improving marriages* should have, in the ministry programme of churches? Why? How?

3. Sometimes the personalities of husband and wife are such that she definitely 'wears the trousers', and in many respects takes the lead in the relationship. They may both be perfectly happy with this pattern. Should we tell them that it is against Scripture, and they should try to change?

Marriage and family life in New Testament times

Jewish and Gentile views were on the whole very similar here. For both, the good order and stability of society as a whole depended upon well-ordered and stable households within society, and the order of both depended upon *men*. The world's first democracy was ancient Athens, they tell us, but only property-owning males, the heads of households, had the vote in this democracy! Women, slaves and men without property had no vote. So society reflected the household, and vice versa: at the head of each was the *ruling male*.

The Greek philosopher Aristotle wrote, 'The rule of the household is a monarchy, for every house is under one head'. And following him many Greek and Roman authors wrote about household management based on this principle of the *male monarch*. The Jewish historian Josephus found the same pattern taught in the Old Testament: 'The woman, it (*the Law*) says, is in all things inferior to the man. Let her accordingly be obedient, not for her humiliation, but that she may be directed; for God has given authority to the man'. And the Jewish philosopher, Philo of Alexandria (a contemporary of Paul), wrote, 'Wives must be in servitude to their husbands, a servitude not imposed by violent ill-treatment but promoting obedience in all things'. The three relationships about which Paul writes here in Ephesians – with wives, with children, and with slaves – were regarded by everyone as the three basic areas in which the man must be 'monarch' in his household.

Of course this did not necessarily mean *lack of love* between husband and wife. It is interesting to find some powerful expressions of the value of married love, even within this male supremacy. The Roman philosopher Musonius Rufus, for example (also contemporary with Paul), wrote that 'in marriage there must be above all perfect companionship and mutual love of husband and wife, both in health and sickness and under all conditions ... each striving to outdo the other in devotion'. But Dr Andrew Lincoln (from whose commentary I have taken all these quotations) comments that Musonius also simply *assumed* 'that men are the rulers and superior while women are the ruled and inferior'.

That is the background to Ephesians! The vital question is, does Paul simply repeat this model of marriage, by using the same words 'head' and 'submit', or does he radically re-model it? We cannot fully answer this question until we have studied through to the end of the 'Household Code' (6:9) but *One way of handling 'Headship'* (p. 160) has a few suggestions.

Ephesians 5:25–30

Specially for him

The word 'as' is vital again as Paul turns to the *husband*. He too must pattern his love for his wife and his ministry to her on the relationship between Christ and the church.

Taking verses 22–30 as a whole, it is fascinating to count the number of times in which the words 'as' or 'in the same way' draw a comparison between the two relationships – Christ and the church, and husband and wife. I make it six. Paul really rubs the point home! Some writers argue that Paul is using *marriage* to illustrate *Christ and the church* – but surely it is the other way round. He is telling us to *shape our marriages on the 'marriage' between Christ and his Bride, the church*.

Verses 26–27 picture the church as a bride being prepared for her wedding. Strangely, she is being prepared by her husband-to-be! In his love for her, Christ works to make his Bride as beautiful as she can be. Paul makes three points about this love – about its *quality*, its *purpose*, and its *surprising object*. And in each case he applies it to Christian husbands.

Its *quality* is self-sacrifice (verse 25). We have already seen how unusual this idea was in the world of Paul's time. Only fools would sacrifice themselves. Paul is reminding husbands of what he wrote in 5:2, where he told *all* the Ephesians, not just the men, to 'walk in love, just as Christ loved us and gave himself up for us as a fragrant offering and sacrifice to God'. So the quality of a Christian husband's love does *not* include holding onto power, position or prestige, but sacrificing all that for the sake of his wife. That's how a Christian 'head' will rule. For the background in the teaching of Jesus, see Mark 10:42–45.

Its *purpose* is the growth of the loved one (verses 26–28). Verses 26–27 are a most moving picture of the sheer delight that Christ takes in his church – the delight that led him to sacrifice himself for her. That delight includes a longing to see her grow into the best that she can be, in fact to become all that God wants her to be. It all boils down to the last three words in verse 27: he longs for the church to be 'holy and blameless', which is exactly what God has planned for us according to Ephesians 1:4.

Husbands likewise should long for their wives to grow in holiness, and should help them to do that. But I believe that the chief thought here is *delight in personal development and fulfilment*. Modelled on Jesus the head of the church, the Christian husband is thrilled at every way in which his wife grows, fulfils her potential, exercises her gifts, realizes all the capacities within her. This arises from the picture of the Bride in verse 27. Just as, on her wedding day, a girl seeks to be *as beautiful as she can possibly be*, so her Christian husband will long for her *maturity in Christ*, wanting to see her full potential brought out, and her gifts and ministries developed completely.

Its *surprising object* is the husband himself (verses 28b–30)! In verse 28 Paul begins a train of thought which is leading up to the quotation of the famous passage about marriage in verse 31. The climax of that quotation is the last two words: 'one flesh'. As we shall see, Paul was clearly amazed by this description of marriage. Two people become 'one flesh'! Here in verse 28 he draws a conclusion from it for the husband: 'He who loves his wife loves himself'. If they are 'one flesh', then this must be so.

But before quoting that text from Genesis, Paul draws the *same thought* out of his comparison with Christ and the church. The church is 'the body of Christ'. We are 'members – literally, *limbs* – of his body' (verse 30). So, in nourishing and caring for his body, the church, Christ too is *caring for his own flesh*, lavishing love on an object which is not separate from himself, but in a real sense *part of himself*. Some scholars shy away from finding this thought here – it seems so dramatic. Jesus, *loving himself* as he loves the church?

Well, you must make your own mind up as you think about this passage!

We could put it a different way and say that *the church is as precious to Christ as his own life.* Yes, literally: he died for her. And this must be how the Christian husband thinks and feels about his wife.

Questions

1. All readers who are husbands know what they ought to think about or discuss at this point! *How do you match up?*
2. What can husbands do, practically, to enable their wives to develop their full potential as people? How might this goal affect the way husbands order their lives?
3. What are the main differences between this understanding of marriage, and the view which people tend to have in the culture round you? What particular difficulties do Christian marriages face in working out this ideal?

Ephesians 5:31–33

Specially for both

Husband and wife are 'one flesh' together, says Paul. This is a 'great mystery' with a great challenge attached!

Paul brings this passage on marriage to a powerful climax here, with his quotation of Genesis 2:24 in verse 31: 'For this reason a man will leave his father and mother and be united to his wife, and the two will become one flesh'. In Genesis, 'for this reason' refers back to the previous verse, where Adam rejoices over the creation of Eve: 'This is now bone of my bones and flesh of my flesh; she shall be called "woman", for she was taken out of man' (Gen. 2:23). So 'one flesh' in Genesis 2:24 refers to the origin of woman as part of the man's body.

Is that what Paul is thinking of, here in Ephesians? 'For this reason' could remind us of the original, Genesis, reason for 'one flesh', or it could fit into Paul's train of thought in Ephesians and refer back to verse 30: 'We are members of his body! *For this reason*, a man will leave his father and mother and be united to his wife ...'.

This second way of understanding 'for this reason' would be revolutionary. Paul would be saying, 'Forget about Genesis. Let me tell you the *real* reason for marriage. This "one flesh" union of husband and wife actually *results from* membership of the Body of Christ!' This thought would need careful unpacking, but there are two good reasons for thinking that this is what Paul has in mind:

- Firstly, he does not introduce this quotation in any way, with 'as it is written' or some equivalent. He just lets the quotation flow straight into his argument, as if he was not disturbed by the thought that it would be taken in close connection with verse 30.

● And secondly, when he comments on 'one flesh' in verse 32, he calls it a 'great mystery' and immediately applies it to 'Christ and the church'! So, clearly, he thought that there was a close connection between the 'one flesh' union of husband and wife, and the union of Christ and the church.

Here is a series of statements, which I think summarize what Paul is teaching here:

● 'One flesh' refers to far more than just sex. The *sexual* union of husband and wife is like the outer sign of a much deeper union. In the Bible there is no sharp dividing-line between our *bodies* and the other parts of us, mind, heart, spirit etc. We don't come in parts, like a house with separate rooms, and only inter-connecting doors between them. We are like oak trees – the bit you can see rests upon and is one with all the rest, the massive root-system which is out of sight.

● So 'one flesh' is a 'great mystery', because it seems to say that, in marriage, two people merge with each other. Marriage does not just mean a joining of *bodies*, but a joining of *persons*. How can this be? How can two human beings become 'one' with each other, while still remaining individuals? This is the 'mystery' that puzzles Paul.

● He solves the puzzle by thinking of Christ and the church. Here we have just the same problem at first sight. How can Christ be the head, united to this body of human beings here on earth? How can the church be 'in' Christ – as Paul has so often put it? 'But I am talking about Christ and the church' (verse 32) would be better translated, 'But I say that this "one flesh" refers to Christ and the church'. *Only in the light of 'Christ and the church' can we make sense of this mysterious Scriptural statement about marriage.*

● So only *in Christ* is this 'one flesh' union of two human beings really possible. People can have a stab at it, outside of Christ, but in the long run *shared membership of his body* (verse 30) is the only basis for this deep-down union of spirit, heart, mind and body.

- Why? Because God plans to make us *all* one with each other in the 'one body' of Christ (4:4). This 'one body' is the foretaste of a *reunited universe*, with everything summed up in Christ (1:10). Husband and wife, by becoming 'one flesh', take a step towards that wonderful unity of all things, *yet to take place in Christ*.

- And there is also a practical reason why real marriage is only possible 'in Christ': only *in Christ* will the husband love his wife *as himself* (verse 33) – that is, protect and nourish her with all the energy of his instinct for *self*-preservation, because she is really his own body (verse 28). And only *in Christ* will the wife 'fear' her husband (verse 33, literal translation), which means that she will treat him with as much care, devotion and delight as if she were serving Christ himself. ('Fear' in verse 33 looks back to 'in the fear of Christ' in verse 21.)

Questions

1. Look back at the question which is probably prompting Paul all through this passage (see above, p. 149–50): is marriage in conflict with church membership? How can we tie them together, in practice?

2. The message of the popular press is that 'a good sex life' is essential for a good marriage. Do you agree? What does this passage say about sex?

3. How would you minister to a single person who felt troubled about his or her singleness?

One way of handling 'Headship'

Look back to the third question on p. 152 above. Opinions are divided about this. Some think that, as the 'head' of the marriage, husbands should lovingly take the lead in the relationship, and wives should lovingly and loyally *follow* the lead set by their husbands, even if they are leading unwisely. But others think that the comparison with *Christ and the church* blows this leader-follower pattern sky-high. In this note I will simply describe how I have found it helpful to understand Paul's teaching – so that readers can work out their own understanding of Paul in disagreement with me, if necessary!

The picture is made more complicated by 1 Corinthians 11:2–16, where Paul writes more broadly about men and women in the church (not just about husbands and wives). For there he begins by saying, 'Now I want you to realise that the head of every man is Christ, and the head of the woman is man, and the head of Christ is God' (1 Cor. 11:3). So it seems that the husband-wife relationship in marriage is the same as the general man-woman relationship in the church. In both, the man is the 'head', for Paul.

Clearly the vital thing is to understand what he meant by this metaphor, 'head'. Here are my four personal convictions about this.

'Head' does not mean 'authority over'. In fact, it doesn't *mean* anything. As a metaphor, it can only *suggest* – and we have to work out what it is suggesting, in each case. 'Head' can certainly suggest 'authority over', and does so in Ephesians 1:22, where Jesus is described as 'head over all things'. But here it is the word 'over' which confirms the note of 'authority'. Appearing on its own, 'head' can suggest many other things as well, as we have already seen in the section on *Christ, the Head of the Body*. And I am convinced that, here in Ephesians 5:23, it suggests some of these other meanings and does not put Christian husbands in a position of authority over their wives.

The following points give my reasons for this conviction:

Paul revolutionizes the other 'household' relationships, also. As we shall see, in the case of parents and children, and of masters and slaves (6:1–4, 5–9), Paul handles things in his own special way. First he seems to say 'Yes' to the usual social patterns, putting parents and masters in positions of authority. But then his actual teaching *revolutionizes* the relationship. He will tell parents that they may not give their children *their own* teaching, but *the Lord's* (6:4). And he will tell slave-owners that they must be as ready to *serve* their slaves as to *receive their service* ('do the same to them', 6:9).

In both cases, the revolution comes from Jesus Christ. Old relationships are turned upside-down, when *parents* know that they too must grow up to maturity in Christ (4:13), and *masters* know that they too have a master in heaven (6:9)! I think that the same happens in the case of husbands and wives. The old *language* of 'headship' and 'submission' is still used, but its meaning is transformed. Husband and wife now belong together to the body of Christ, where the rule is 'submit to one another out of reverence for Christ' (5:21).

Paul's use of 'head' for the husband does not undermine complete mutuality. In other words, even though Paul calls the husband 'head', he clearly regards husband and wife as equal partners in marriage. Each belongs totally to the other. He gives himself 100 per cent for her, imitating the sacrifice of Jesus (5:25). In loving her, he loves himself, because they become 'one flesh' in Christ. Paul puts it slightly differently in 1 Corinthians 7:4: 'The wife's body does not belong to her alone but also to her husband. In the same way, the husband's body does not belong to him alone but also to his wife'. Here, 'belong to' is literally 'have authority over'. For Paul, both husband and wife 'have authority over' each other's bodies.

And the same is true of men and women more generally, in 1 Corinthians 11. There too, even though Paul calls man 'the head of the woman', he goes on to write, 'In the Lord, however, woman is not independent of man, nor is man independent of woman. For as woman came from man, so also man is born of woman. But everything comes from God' (verses 11–12). Men and women are mutually dependent before God.

So why, then, does Paul continue to use the metaphor of 'head' to describe the male side of this relationship? I suggested one answer above (point 2) – he does not want to *attack* the normal patterns of family relationships, but rather to *subtly transform* them by the Gospel. So he continues using the usual words, but connects them with a whole new way of understanding the relationships: 'just as Christ ... in the Lord ... their Master and yours!' (5:25, 6:1, 6:9).

But another answer lies in the flexibility of metaphors. The same metaphor can suggest different things in different contexts. For instance, in Ephesians 6:12 'struggle' points to our spiritual battle, by prayer and faith, against the forces of evil, but in Philippians 1:30 Paul applies the same metaphor to *coping with suffering*. So we must ask, if the metaphor 'head' applied to husbands can no longer suggest 'authority over', what does it suggest instead?

'Head' in Ephesians 5:23 suggests four things, I believe: responsibility, incompleteness, intimacy and commitment. These four things are all connected, and all arise out of 'as Christ is the head of the church, his body, of which he is the Saviour':

● Jesus has taken upon himself the responsibility, the *task*, of saving the church and bringing us to glory.

● He has done this by giving himself for us, and uniting himself to us, so that he is incomplete without us, like a head without a body.

● United to us in this way, we are 'one flesh' with him (5:31–32), and so in a relationship of deep intimacy with him, just as heads and bodies are 'one flesh' with each other.

● To enable his body to grow and to function properly, he not only gives himself for us, but also showers gifts upon us, his church. He 'feeds and cares for us' (5:29), in total commitment.

Incompleteness and *intimacy* are the two sides of one coin, and so are *responsibility* and *commitment*. In all these respects the 'headship' of Christ is the pattern for the 'headship' of the Christian husband. The ideas of 'rule' and 'authority over' have no place here! And the same applies, I believe, to 1 Corinthians 11:2–16. That is a difficult passage and we cannot look at it in detail. But when Paul says that 'the head of Christ is God', he cannot mean that God rules over Christ. On the contrary, God *shares* his rule with Christ, as we see later in 1 Corinthians 15:24–28. There, it is the risen Christ who 'reigns' on God's behalf until the End, when he will hand over the kingdom to God and submit to him. Again, intimacy and mutuality are the name of the game.

I believe that this understanding of 'headship' is not only Scriptural, but also pastorally right. It allows married couples to be themselves, and to work out whatever pattern suits them, within this total commitment to each other's well-being. It releases husbands from having to adopt a leadership role which does not come naturally to them. Likewise it releases wives from having to adopt a submissive role, if this is not their 'style'! It encourages completely mutual decision-making, and a sense of fundamental partnership, belonging and dependence.

This does not mean that the roles of each partner are exactly the same. Of the four components of meaning in 'head', outlined above, three apply equally to both, but one is particularly for husbands, I believe. Incompleteness, intimacy and commitment apply just as much to wives as to husbands, but *responsibility* attaches particularly to husbands. As the 'head', the husband has a particular responsibility to ensure that his wife is growing to maturity as a person in Christ, and that she is discovering, developing and exercising her gifts and ministries within the body of Christ, whatever they are. On the whole, we Christian husbands have not done well at this, especially at times and places where women have not been *allowed* to exercise certain gifts and ministries within the church! But that's another story ...

Ephesians 6:1–4

Children and parents

As he continues his focus on special relationships within the church, Paul does something very unusual by talking directly to the children in the Ephesian church. Oh, and to their parents too.

I mentioned above that there are other examples of 'family advice' from various philosophers and writers around the time of Paul and earlier. *In none of them are the children addressed directly as Paul does here*. In fact, wives and slaves are not addressed directly, either. All the advice is given to the male head of the household, the one responsible for managing the women, children and slaves.

So Paul breaks new ground by speaking directly to the children in the Ephesian church. And this in itself says something very important about the place of children in the church. They are not adults-in-waiting. Even as children, they are full members of the church, with a special role to fulfil (verses 1–2) and a special need of encouragement and support (verse 4).

The two phrases 'in the Lord' (verse 1) and 'of the Lord' (verse 4) point us in this direction. They put the relationship between children and parents onto a different basis. No longer is the relationship merely biological. They are now related to each other 'in the Lord', and this transforms the picture, just as it transforms the relationship between husband and wife. From a purely biological perspective, parents are superior and have absolute rights over their children. In some societies these rights are restrained by law. But in the Greek society of Ephesus the restraints were not great. Parents could 'expose' unwanted children at birth – that is, they could just abandon them to die – and no one would object. In many societies today, parents are allowed to do this *before* birth, and few people object – because they think just of the *biological* side of the relationship with their unborn children.

But the relationship Paul describes is not biological. To use a technical word, it is *christological* – bound up with *Christ* – and so children and parents need to see each other through new eyes:

- Children must obey their parents 'in the Lord', that is, because they and their parents *belong together* to the Lord Jesus, must *live together* as he wants, as fellow-members of his body, and *grow together* to maturity in him (4:13). We *all* need to grow, not just our children!

- Parents must bring their children up 'in the training and instruction of the Lord' (verse 4), that is, they must set aside *their own* ambitions for their children and train them to be *what the Lord wants them to be*. They are just passing on instruction from someone else, not trying to shape their children into little replicas of themselves!

This is the *Christian* understanding of childhood. Alongside us, our children are fellow-members of the body of Christ, equal with us before the Lord, but in need of special nurture, love and teaching on the path toward the goal of *maturity in Christ* – the goal we share with them. No wonder Paul actually says more to the children than to their parents.

So, in more detail, what does he actually teach here?

- Children must obey. This is how they will learn the wonderful quality of *self-control*, so basic to Christian discipleship. Of course we parents must make sure that their obedience is not harmful to them – and Paul tells us so in verse 4. 'Do not exasperate your children' gives the necessary balance. Parents can abuse their authority, and produce a deep-seated resentment in children who are always being forced into submission. That's not obedience! In the parallel passage in Colossians Paul writes, 'do not embitter your children, or they will become discouraged' (Col. 3:21). Children need to *be encouraged* to obey as part of their response to *Christ*, and not *be forced* to obey as a response just to *their parents*.

Then Paul gives two reasons for obedience:

● 'For this is right' (verse 1b). Obedience is *right* because God has commanded it. Paul quotes the fifth commandment (Ex. 20:12; Deut. 5:16). Clearly this is not one of the 'commandments and regulations' which have been abolished by Christ (see Eph. 2:15)! Paul thought that only the parts of the law which made Israel distinct from the Gentiles had been abolished. That is exactly the point he is making in Ephesians 2:11–22! On the other hand, the parts of the law which expressed the mind and heart of God were as true as ever. This is important for understanding Paul's second reason for obedience:

● 'that it may go well with you, and that you may enjoy long life on the earth' (verse 3). Originally, of course, this promised Israel long life 'in the *land* the Lord your God is giving you' (Deut. 5:16 – the same word can mean both 'earth' and 'land'). But in line with his principle that God has broken down the distinction between Jews and Gentiles, Paul finds a broader meaning in the promise. 'Long life' is a symbol for *well-being and maturity*. If children will learn the self-discipline of obedience, they will grow to the full maturity which is our greatest calling as human beings – see 4:13!

Questions

1. What is the attitude of your church toward the children in it? Do you think Paul would approve?

2. What are the particular challenges and obstacles in your society which make it difficult for parents to bring their children up 'in the training and instruction of the Lord'? How, practically, can these be overcome?

3. What is your church doing, to support *Christian family life* today? What more could be done?

167

Ephesians 6:5–9

Slaves and masters

The relationship between slaves and masters is also transformed by Christ, especially when he is *shared* by masters and slaves together.

As he turns to the third family relationship, Paul once again departs from the usual practice by addressing the slaves first, and much more fully than the masters. This is remarkable, when we consider the status of slaves in society at that time. For some information on this, see *Slavery in New Testament times*, p. 170.

This section is a little different from the other two because the slaves may have non-Christian masters. But even so, *Jesus makes a very big difference to the relationship*. The little word 'as' or 'like', so important in the section on wives and husbands, appears here again (verses 5, 6, 7). What does Paul teach? In four ways, the Christian slave will have a new attitude to his life and work:

- *A new loyalty* (verse 5) The vital phrase is the last one, 'just as you would obey Christ'. A non-Christian slave can be loyal, but only the Christian slave can have *this* loyalty to his or her master!

- *A new master* (verse 6) Who are they actually serving? In the long run, they are not serving their human master at all, but they are 'slaves of Christ'. This is actually how Paul describes himself at the beginning of two of his letters – 'a slave of Christ Jesus' (Rom. 1:1; Phil. 1:1). So, in a sense, their loyalty *has* been stolen away and given to another. Now, like all other Christians, it is *God's* will they want to do (see 5:17).

- *A new spirit* (verse 7) 'Serve wholeheartedly', says Paul. 'Whole-heartedly' is literally 'with good will, enthusiasm'. And once again what gives this new spirit is the sense of *who it is for*. They are doing it all *not* for their human masters, but for 'the Lord'. They must bring to their work all the enthusiasm they would feel, if they were directly serving Jesus himself – because in fact they are!

- *A new motivation* (verse 8) A non-Christian slave might be very anxious to *get a better deal* for himself or herself – to improve prospects and rewards. But the Christian slave has a completely different horizon. He has his eyes fixed on a much greater reward! And this is something that puts him on a level with all other Christians: 'whether he is slave or free', the Lord will give the reward deserved for the good he does. So, says Paul – concentrate on doing good, and earning that reward!

Finally Paul turns to the masters (verse 9). 'Treat your slaves in the same way', he says – literally, 'do the same things to them'. What? Can Paul really mean it? Is he actually telling the masters to serve their slaves in the same way as the slaves serve them? Well, not *quite* ... because he goes on to say 'do not threaten them', and this suggests that the masters are still in charge. But on the other hand, he gets very close to saying this. He *certainly* says that, before the Lord, there is no difference between them and their slaves ('there is no favouritism with him'). He is equally the Lord of all. And so *they, the masters, must be as committed to the well-being and growth of their slaves as they are to any other members of the body of Christ.*

That is the difference that Jesus makes!

Questions

1. Being *employed* is obviously very different from being a *slave*. Do you think we can apply Paul's teaching here to the relationship between employers and their employees?
2. Many Christians feel disappointed that they spend all their working time doing 'unspiritual' jobs – in an office, a factory, a shop. What do you think Paul might want to say to them?

3. Are there modern forms of slavery in the world today? What should we be doing about them? Should we try to abolish such slavery? Would Paul tell these modern 'slaves' to obey their masters as he does here?

Slavery in New Testament times

Slavery was very widespread in the first century. It has been estimated that one-third of the population of Greece and Italy were slaves. Virtually all households had slaves living as part of the family – and of course the slaves might have children of their own (although the law did not permit *marriage* between slaves). They might work within the house, cooking or cleaning, or outside in the family business, and they might actually be highly educated, and have responsible positions – for instance, teaching the children or administering a large estate. Some masters were of course cruel and female slaves especially might be exploited sexually, but this was not always so.

However, even if they had much responsibility, slaves had no legal rights whatsoever. So far as the law was concerned, they were just property, not people. This meant that their lives were very insecure. Perhaps just a year or so before Ephesians was written, this had been vividly shown in Rome. Paul must have known about the dreadful occasion on which the 400 slaves of Pedanius Secundus were all executed, just because one of them had murdered his master in a fit of anger. The law said they should all be executed for the crime, so they were. The Roman Senate approved the order, because 'nowadays our huge households are international. They include every alien religion – or none at all. The only way to keep down this scum is by intimidation!' (These are the words of one of the senators, recorded by the Roman historian Tacitus.)

Slaves were expected to give absolute loyalty to their master, even to the extent of adopting his religion. Sometimes this worked for the Gospel, as for instance in the case of the Philippian jailor, who was accompanied by his entire household when he became a Christian! (See Acts 16:30–34.) Here in Ephesians, it is interesting that Paul *assumes* that Christian masters will have Christian slaves (verse 9).

But of course it did not work the other way round. Many slaves became Christians in the early years of the church (see 1 Cor. 1:26–27), and if they were departing from their master's religion they could be accused of disloyalty. In response to this threat, Paul's advice was, 'Show that being a Christian makes you an even better slave!' As he puts it in 1 Tim. 6:1, 'All who are under the yoke of slavery should consider their masters worthy of full respect, so that God's name and our teaching may not be slandered'.

Families: God's second best?

Now we must come back to the question we asked at the beginning of this section on marriage and family life (see above, pp. 149–50): how can commitment to *marriage, family and employment* fit in with this *membership of the body of Christ* in which we find our whole reason for existence? As we saw, this is a cause of conflict and tension for many Christians.

Some scholars think that Paul contradicts himself. They suggest that, when he describes our life in Christ in chapters 1–4, he has his head firmly stuck in the clouds; so when he starts to give practical advice about Christian living, as he knows he must, he really does not know what to say and simply adopts ideas from various sources, both Greek and Jewish. In this 'Household Code' (they suggest), Paul is just repeating the kind of advice given by various other writers, and we must recognize that *it doesn't really fit in* with his teaching about 'the body of Christ' at all.

But surely this cannot be right! We only have to point to Paul's repeated use of the word 'as' to tell us that we must relate to each other 'as' Christ relates to us: nine times in 5:22 – 6:9. And there are another four points where he makes the same connection without using the word 'as' – so on *thirteen occasions in twenty-one verses Paul expresses his own feeling that this 'Household Code' does not contradict his teaching about the church as the body of Christ, but comes straight out of it!*

How? We have seen the answer as we have looked at these wonderful passages.

- On marriage: he has taught that the 'one flesh' union of husband and wife only makes sense *in Christ*, because in him they can begin to discover in their marriage that unity of all things which God plans for the universe.

- On parenthood: he has told parents and children that their relationship is primarily 'in the Lord', and *obedience* and *instruction* must all be in him.

- On slavery: he has told slaves and masters that they both belong first of all to the Lord, the Master in heaven, so that earthly masters must 'do the same things' for their slaves as the slaves do for them!

- I believe that we can say three things about Paul's teaching here: about his *strategy*, his *theology*, and his *practice*.

Paul's strategy is to appear to say 'Yes' to the usual pattern, but actually to undermine it. This is his strategy also in the letter to Philemon, which is also concerned with slavery. One of the older commentators on Philemon, the famous Bishop Lightfoot, wrote, 'Slavery is never directly attacked as such, but principles are inculcated which must prove fatal to it'. Paul never directly *tells* Philemon to release Onesimus from slavery. He leaves it to Philemon to make up his own mind (see Philem. 6). But it is pretty clear that the old master–slave relationship has been blown sky-high, because Onesimus is now 'a dear brother' (verse 10)!

It is just the same here in Ephesians – not only with masters and slaves, but with the other two relationships as well. How can 'head' and 'submit' mean 'rule' and 'obey', when *Christ and the church* are the model and pattern? And how can parents go on thinking of their children as their *biological property*, if their duty is to pass on *the Lord's* training and instruction to them?

Paul's theology is to make family life the arena of Christian service for those called to it. Yes, our primary membership is of the body of Christ. Within that body, we find our whole reason for existence. We are called to undertake 'works of service, so that the body of Christ may be built up' (4:12). But if we are also called to marriage and family life, then that is where our service is to be *focused*. The *call* to service is general, the *arena* of service is particular. Husbands and wives must focus their service on each other, and on their children.

Many Christians, especially those in leadership, need to be reminded of this! And perhaps those around them have a particular responsibility, gently to point out if they are neglecting their families for the sake of the church. Paul gives no easy answer to the practical difficulties here. But he says very firmly to us that *the family is where we live in Christ*, if God has called us to marriage.

And the same applies to our jobs. *Whatever Christian slaves do, they are serving the Lord*: that is his message. We can apply this to ourselves. To do our work for the Lord, whatever it is ... that is the Christian way.

Paul's practice is to put the Lord first, in every area of his life. Did he change his mind between 1 Corinthians and Ephesians? He seems so much more positive about marriage in Ephesians. He may have changed a little! But the basic principle is the same:

- *Because he put the Lord first in his life*, he remained unmarried so that he would be free to please the Lord without distraction (1 Cor. 7:32). Paul never felt a second-class Christian because of his unmarried status. Far from it, he boasted of the fulfilling life he had (Phil. 1:21). This is still a call that God gives to many of his children.

- *Because they put the Lord first in their lives*, Christians who marry will sacrifice themselves for each other and for their children, so that they may grow up into Christ, the Head. This is a call that God gives to many other of his children!

Either way, the Lord is our primary loyalty.

10

SPIRITUAL WARFARE
Ephesians 6:10–24

Setting the scene

This famous passage brings the letter to a most powerful conclusion. It picks up the main themes of the letter and weaves them together in an inspiring final *exhortation*.

This passage is one of the most important in the whole Bible on the subject of 'Spiritual Warfare'. This has gripped the minds of many Christians in recent years. Not surprisingly, therefore, many books have been written on this passage! I shall not refer to any of them in what follows, because readers of this *Bible Guide* may have read different books to those I have read, or none of them at all. However, it is worth bearing in mind some of the things that are being taught, on the basis of this passage and others:

- 'Territorial spirits' – the powers of evil are arranged in a hierarchy, with individual demons at the bottom of the pyramid assigned to small locations on the earth – towns, streets, even individual houses.

- 'Warfare Prayer' – as a vital first step in evangelism, we should identify the names of the spirits that rule over the area, and pray against them in the name of Christ.

- 'Prayer walking' – we can 'take' an area for Christ by marching through it in prayer, exorcizing the spirits that rule it from the past, and claiming it for the Lord.

We cannot look at all this teaching in detail. We will concentrate on simply *listening to Paul*, and then in a brief section on *Spiritual Warfare Today* (p. 186) we will think further about it.

Ephesians 6:10–13

Standing against the enemy

Paul urges us to put on God's armour to protect us in the battle against the forces of evil which try to make us fall.

'Finally, be strong in the Lord and in his mighty power' (6:10). Bringing his letter to a conclusion, Paul returns to the theme of *power* which was so important in chapters 1–3. There he first of all *prayed* that we might know how great God's power is for us, and then illustrated it with the resurrection of Jesus (1:19ff). God's power has raised Jesus to a position of authority over all other 'powers', and now we have been raised *with* Christ and are 'seated with him in the heavenly realms' (2:6). What does it mean in practice to be raised above all these 'powers' in Christ? Paul went on to pray again – this time that we would be 'strengthened with power through his Spirit' in our 'inner being' (3:16), because that is where the battle must be fought.

If we can be strengthened and win the battle in our 'inner being', then we will be able to live as Paul has told us to in chapters 4–6. We will be able to stand firm against false ideas (4:14), and to go on being made new in 'the spirit of your minds' (4:23). We will be able to preserve our unity, control our speech, live lives of purity in a corrupt world, sacrifice ourselves in love for each other as Jesus did for us, and be filled with the Spirit in our worship. Our family lives will be transformed. *But none of this will happen, unless the resurrecting power of God himself is an every-day reality for us.*

Why? Because, as the Ephesians knew only too well, the powers of evil are too great for us to conquer on our own. Converted out of the pagan background pictured by Luke in Acts 19, they knew the powers of evil long before they knew the power of God. And they knew how easily they could be sucked back into the wickedness around them. Paul knew that too. And so he tells them: you need to 'be strong in the Lord and in his mighty power' (verse 10)!

He really rubs the point in:

- *What they should do* (verse 11a); put on God's armour

- *The purpose* (verse 11b): so that they can stand firm

- *The reason* (verse 12): because the enemy is so strong

- *What they should do* (verse 13a): put on God's armour

- *The purpose* (verse 13b): so that they can stand firm

So what does Paul teach us here?

We need weapons to match the enemy's. The devil attacks us with 'schemes' (verse 11) – that is, cunning plans designed to deceive us, and to make us fall into sin and disunity. Paul has given an example of a 'scheme' in 4:26–27: 'Do not let the sun go down while you are still angry, and do not give the devil a foothold'. The devil will *feed* feelings of anger, because they can lead to disunity in the body of Christ, and to hatred instead of love. Against attacks like this there is only one defence – the armour of God.

As we shall see 'the armour of God' is not just 'the armour God *gives*', but also 'the armour God *wears*'. It is his own *personal* armour, which he shares with us. Nothing less than this will do, against the power of the devil.

We need to know the enemy's strength. This is essential, in any war! So in verse 12 Paul reminds us of *the awesome power of the devil's forces*: we are fighting 'against the rulers, against the authorities, against the powers of this dark world, against the spiritual forces of evil in the heavenly realms'. Paul is probably not describing different types of demonic power with each of these phrases. He is just piling up names and descriptions – four of them, in fact, gradually getting longer and more horrifying. One of them, the word translated 'powers' (which actually means 'world powers' or 'world rulers'), was used of the goddess Artemis in magic spells at this time.

How can we 'stand' against such dreadful forces? Only with *God's* strength and armour.

We need stamina for the battle. More than anything else, a soldier needs to be physically fit. The best-equipped soldier in the world will be no use in battle, if he is panting for breath after 100 metres! He needs *stamina*, the ability to keep going *however hard the battle gets* ('when the day of evil comes'), and *however long the battle lasts* ('after you have done everything, to stand'). He needs to stand up against a sudden, sharp attack, and to keep marching solidly day after day. And so do we! Only God's armour will give us this double kind of stamina for the fight, to keep us *steady* and to keep us *going*.

Questions

1. 'Our struggle is not against flesh and blood' (verse 12). Does Paul mean it? Did he have no *human* enemies? Why does he say this? How can we apply this to ourselves?

2. 'Be strong ... put on ...': Paul is talking to the Ephesians *as a group* here, rather than to each individual Christian in the Ephesian church. Does the devil attack us individually, or as churches? How can *churches* 'be strong ... put on ...'?

3. What kind of 'day of evil' do you think Paul has in mind, in verse 13? See 5:16. When do we feel the power of the devil's schemes most of all? What can help us at such times?

Ephesians 6:14–17

God's armour for us to wear

Paul describes the six pieces of armour which will keep us firm in the fight.

This is *God's* armour. There are two important passages where God himself is described as wearing parts of this armour:

- Isaiah 59:15–18: 'The LORD looked and was displeased that there was no justice ... So ... he put on righteousness as his breastplate, and the helmet of salvation on his head; he put on the garments of vengeance and wrapped himself in zeal as in a cloak. According to what they have done, so will he repay wrath to his enemies ...'

- Wisdom 5:17–20: 'The Lord will take his zeal as his whole armour, and will arm all creation to repel his enemies; he will put on righteousness as a breastplate, and wear impartial justice as a helmet; he will take holiness as an invincible shield, and sharpen stern wrath for a sword ...'

The book of Wisdom, while not part of our Bibles, was widely known in New Testament times, and helps us see what Paul means by 'the armour of God'. As I put it above, it is not just the armour he *gives*, but also the armour he himself *wears*. And he wears it in order to defeat 'his enemies' – just the *same* enemies as the ones we are fighting against.

The list of six pieces of armour falls into two groups:

- Four pieces we *take* (verses 14–16)

- Two pieces we *receive* (verse 17)

181

The word 'take' at the beginning of verse 17 is usually translated 'receive', and a close look at the last two pieces of armour reveals that they are different: we cannot take them up for ourselves, but can only depend on God to give them to us (which he is very ready to do!).

- *The belt of truth*   'Truth' has a double meaning, and in *both* senses it forms our foundation-garment, underlying all the rest. We can illustrate the double meaning by thinking of the two places where truth can be:
  - in our *heads*, truth is *a quality of our minds*, affecting both what we know and the way we speak (see Eph. 1:13, 4:15, 20);
  - in our *hearts*, truth is *a quality of our character*, affecting the way we behave (see Eph. 4:24, 5:9). We need both!

- *The breastplate of righteousness*   Probably Paul is thinking of the way we behave here, too. 'Righteousness' is one of the great qualities of the new nature which God gives us in Christ, according to Ephesians 4:24 and 5:9. If we will keep this righteousness around us – not letting it slip, treasuring it – then the devil will not be able to get at us.

- *The shoes of the Gospel of peace*   We will be ready for war if we have peace on our feet! Paul's mind is going back to 2:14–17, 4:3 and all that he has said about the *unity* of the body of Christ. God's whole plan, explained in the Gospel, is to create *one* church which enjoys 'the unity of the Spirit through the bond of peace' (4:3). The devil will try to ruin that peace! And he will succeed – unless the Gospel is firmly fixed on our feet, guiding all our steps.

- *The shield of faith*   Burning arrows caused panic among soldiers by setting their shields on fire, and efforts were made to design shields which would not catch fire. The devil will try to burn down our defences – but the shield of faith will not burn. Paul mentions faith throughout the letter (ten times, in fact – in 1:13, 15, 19; 2:8; 3:12, 17; 4:5, 13; 6:16, 23). It is the *past* (1:13, 2:8), *present* (1:19, 3:12) and *future* (4:13) of the Christian life! Our basic attitude of trust and commitment to the Lord and his way.

- *The helmet of salvation*   Paul has mentioned salvation in 1:13 and in 2:5, 8. In all these places it is clearly something that God alone gives. We cannot work for it or 'take it up' like the shield of faith. All we can do is 'receive' it. But what a thought this is! Soldiering is one of the most dangerous professions in the world. Especially when going into battle, a soldier can have no confidence of survival or 'safety'. But we can! Facing this battle with the devil and all his forces, we can receive from God an *assurance* that we will be kept safe, however hard the fight may be.

- *The sword of the Spirit*   Once again, this is something we can only receive, for this sword is 'the word of God', and we can only speak the words of God himself if he gives them to us. Paul asks the Ephesians to pray that he will receive this gift (6:19)! It is clear that 'the word of God' here does not mean *the Bible*, but *the Gospel* – the word which we speak when we bear witness. When we do that, we want to speak not *our* words, but *God's*.

Questions

1. How many of these pieces of armour are things which we can really only put on *together*, as a whole church?
2. 'Flaming arrows' strike without warning and need urgent action. What sort of things might Paul be thinking of? Has your church or fellowship been hit by any recently?
3. Can you think of ways in which you could use this passage as the basis of a teaching session for the whole church – perhaps using drama?

Ephesians 6:18–20

Constant prayer

A final section on prayer rounds off this letter which has been so full of prayer and praise. Prayer must be the constant attitude of our hearts and lives.

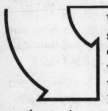 We are in the middle of another of Paul's long sentences here. There is only a light break at the end of verse 16, so the sentence really runs from verse 14 through to the end of verse 20 (113 words). There is certainly no break after verse 17, even though Paul seems to move on to another topic, *prayer*.

This helps us with a puzzle about the last piece of armour, the sword of the Spirit. It is so wonderful to be able to speak the powerful, live-giving words of God himself. When *we* speak, our words fall on deaf ears. But when *God* speaks, unbelief falls away, faith is born, and the hearers rise to new life in Christ!

Paul tells us just to 'receive' the sword of the Spirit – but how can we do this? It is plain that God is anxious to give this Sword. But why are our words so rarely effective and life-giving, full of his power?

This paragraph tells us the answer. Paul just carries straight on, with no break, into this topic of *prayer*. And in verse 19 he asks the Ephesians to pray for him, that he will receive the sword of the Spirit himself, 'that a word may be given to me, when I open my mouth boldly to make known the mystery of the Gospel' (literal translation). He can 'open his mouth' at any time, but unless he then speaks a word from God he will not 'make known the mystery'. People will hear the words, but no *revelation* will take place.

But Paul is the one who was specially appointed to be the channel of this revelation – see 3:2–9! Yet *even he* needs to depend upon the

Lord for the gift of that Spirit-empowered word. And if he needed to, how much more do we!

What's more, he depends on the Ephesians. Prayer binds him together with them, within the body of Christ. So even though he is in prison, they share his life and his ministry through prayer. And even though he is in prison, he can speak the word of God 'with freedom' if God gives him the word to speak! (The word translated 'fearlessly' in NIV is the same as 'freedom' in 3:12.) For 'God's word is not chained!' (2 Tim. 2:9).

So *effective evangelism is born out of prayer* – that is the message of these verses. What kind of prayer? It must be:

● *Sustained* – 'on all occasions' (that is, no opportunity for prayer is missed).

● *Spiritual* – 'in the Spirit' (that is, we pray *knowing* that the Spirit has given us access to God through Christ: see 2:18!).

● *Varied* – 'with all kinds of prayers and requests'. No stereotyped prayers, but enjoying the freshness of continual variety.

● *Sacrificial* – 'be alert and always keep on'. 'Be alert' is the same as 'watch' in Jesus' warning to his disciples, 'Be always on the watch, and pray that you may be able to escape all that is about to happen' (Luke 21:36). With the devil prowling around (see 1 Pet. 5:8), we cannot let our guard slip.

● *Universal* – 'for all the saints'. Prayer binds the whole body of Christ together in love. We *love people* by praying for them.

● *Particular* – 'and also for me'. Paul depends on the Ephesians to empower his ministry by their prayer. The same is true for all who set out to *speak in the name of Christ*.

Paul keeps repeating the word 'all' in these verses. Literally, he writes 'with all prayer ... at all times ... by all perseverance ... for all the saints!' – and we could take these four 'alls' as the pattern for the Christian practice of prayer.

Questions
1. How can we pray effectively 'for all the saints'? What does Paul mean by this?

2. Review your own prayer life, and the prayer life of your church, in the light of Paul's teaching. Be honest. How, practically, could you or the church move forward in growth in this area?

3. In this passage, is Paul thinking mainly of *prayer together with others*, or mainly of *private, individual prayer*? Does this matter? Or is there something special about praying together?

Spiritual Warfare Today

We have studied Ephesians 6:10–20, the most important passage in the Bible on Spiritual Warfare. Before we draw three *positive* conclusions about it, it is important to notice four things that we do *not* find in this passage:

- We do not find evil spirits attached to particular places. There may be some evidence for this elsewhere in the Bible. See the section on Ephesians 3:8–12 above (p. 87). And we could think also of the 'high places' mentioned in the Old Testament, where demons were worshipped. But here, Paul does not tell his readers to find the identity of the demon ruling Ephesus and to 'name' it as they pray against it. This does not seem to occur to him as a possible mission strategy. In fact, such advice would sound like the pagan magical practices which the Ephesian Christians had left behind.

- We do not find a 'hierarchy' of evil powers. Some people suggest that the four phrases in verse 12 are the levels of command in the devil's army, but this is not likely. In fact, there is disagreement about whether 'the rulers' (the first one) are at the top, or the bottom, of the power-structure!

- There is no mention of 'prayer walking', as a strategy for combating the paganism of Ephesus.

- And 'Prayer Warfare' is not directed *at* the powers of evil, but prayer is addressed to *God*, and is about 'the saints'. More on this below.

I am not suggesting that all these things are wrong, just because we do not find them in this passage. I have frequently been on praise marches and taken part in open-air witness. But I believe that some of the current *emphases* in teaching about spiritual warfare perhaps need re-balancing, in the light of the emphases set by Paul here. What is spiritual warfare, according to Ephesians 6:10–20? I am struck by three things:

- Its *personnel*: spiritual warfare is not to be conducted by a few Christians set apart for the purpose, but by *all*. Every one of us is signed up in the army, and must fight.

- Its *purpose*: here is something strange, at first sight. *The purpose of spiritual warfare is not primarily the defeat of the devil and his forces*. All the pieces of armour are *defensive*, except the last one (the sword of the Spirit). Of course, there are times when it is right to tackle the powers of evil *offensively*, for instance in exorcism (as Jesus himself did). But here, the primary purpose of spiritual warfare is *the protection of the church from the 'schemes' of the devil*. And the devil's schemes attack our *behaviour*, or (to use an old-fashioned word) our *morals*. He wants to corrupt us morally – to undermine our truthfulness, compromise our righteousness, destroy our peace, and weaken our faith. So in all these four areas we need the protection of God's armour.

  And the single *offensive* weapon is not primarily meant to defeat the devil, either. The sword of the Spirit is the word of *the Gospel*, directed at other people around us. Of course, every conversion is a defeat for the devil, and the church is meant to be showing God's wisdom to the rulers and powers (3:10). But in the long run it is *God's* job finally to defeat the devil, not ours. We 'stand' in the victory of Jesus.

- Its *powerhouse*: the power behind spiritual warfare is *prayer*. As we pray, so we and 'all the saints' will learn to 'be strong in the Lord and in his mighty power'. Prayer is something to which we need to give absolute priority, according to this passage. It must be the focus of our lives. And, to judge by this letter, it was certainly the focus of Paul's life. He could not stop himself from bursting into prayer, even as he wrote to the Ephesians. His heart spoke and he prayed onto paper – showing us spiritual warfare at work in the very writing of this marvellous letter.

These are the principles of Spiritual Warfare as taught by Paul.

Ephesians 6:21–24

Final greetings from Paul

Paul introduces Tychicus, the bearer of the letter, and sends his final prayer-wishes to the Ephesians.

There was no public postal service in the Roman empire! So sending letters to friends was difficult. But Paul did not let the difficulties stand in his way. He obviously felt very strongly that he *needed* to stay in touch with the churches where he had ministered. And so he recruited people like Tychicus, actually to take the letters he wrote many hundreds of kilometres to their destinations. No wonder he calls Tychicus a 'faithful servant in the Lord' (verse 21).

It looks as though Tychicus took at least two letters with him, Ephesians and Colossians, and that he travelled with Onesimus the slave, who was also carrying a letter from Paul to his master Philemon (see Col. 4:7–9 and Philem. 10).

But Tychicus was not just meant to be a postman. He was also meant to bring personal news of Paul to the Ephesians (verse 21). Paul knows that he cannot expect them to pray intelligently for him (verse 19), unless they know something about his circumstances. Tychicus will give them the raw material for their prayers.

And more. He was not meant to be just a channel of information, either. He was sent to *encourage* them (verse 22). From the way Paul expresses this, it appears that the news and the encouragement are not necessarily linked. He wants Tychicus to 'encourage' the Christians in Ephesus in a general way, not just by telling them encouraging things about Paul.

The ministry of encouragement is very special. Paul lists it as one of the spiritual gifts in Romans 12:8. Someone with this gift leaves those he or she meets feeling closer to Christ, warmed in heart, with their zeal rekindled and their love strengthened. In pastoral ministry, this is the spiritual gift I covet more than any other. It looks as though Tychicus had it! – like Barnabas (Acts 4:36; 11:22–24).

Finally Paul sends a closing prayer-wish to the Ephesians (verses 23–24). It is a mirror of the prayer-wish with which he began the letter, in 1:2: 'Grace and peace to you from God our Father and the Lord Jesus Christ'. Here he puts it the other way round: *Peace* (verse 23) and *grace* (verse 24)!

Peace (verse 23) has been a vital theme of the letter. *It is the central quality of church life, in Ephesians.* Above all else, we must live at peace with each other (4:3), because God has broken down hostility through Christ (2:14–17), and so if we let hostility break out again it is a total denial of all that God has done through the death of his Son.

Here in his concluding prayer-wish Paul adds 'love with faith' to peace. Love and faith (see 1:15) are the qualities which will keep peace alive and well in the church – love towards 'the brothers', and faith towards Christ. 'The brothers', incidentally, are both male and female! Paul is *not* wishing peace only to the male members of the Ephesian church. 'Brothers' can be used with this either-sex meaning.

And grace (verse 24) has been equally important. If peace is the basis of church life, grace is the basis of God's whole action towards us. He treats us not as we deserve, but shows us 'grace' – see 1:6–7; 2:5–8; 4:7. His *grace towards us* is very close in meaning to his *love for us* (see 2:4–5) – and so to love him back is the response which matches grace. This is why Paul's prayer-wish is 'grace to all who love our Lord Jesus Christ'. He creates in us a reflection of his attitude towards us, and we grow into his likeness – see 4:13.

The last phrase in verse 24 is not 'with an undying love' (NIV) but 'in immortality'. This is rather puzzling. How can we love 'in immortality'? I think the point is that our relationship of love with Jesus will break the bounds of death, because we are *already* seated with him in the heavenly places, sharing his resurrection life (2:6).

Questions

1. Can you identify people in your fellowship with the gift of encouragement? How can this gift and ministry be strengthened in your church?

2. What priority should we give to *obtaining news* about Christians and churches in other parts of the world? How well do you think your church does in this respect?

3. Look back over the whole of Ephesians, and review your study of it. Write down, and discuss with others if possible, what you feel God has taught you through it. What practical steps will you take to respond to what God has said?

For further reading

Commentaries
● The *Bible Speaks Today* volume on Ephesians by John R.W. Stott, *The Message of Ephesians: God's New Society* (Leicester, IVP, 1979) is excellent.

● There are several large commentaries on Ephesians for the more adventurous, and the one I recommend most is the 'Word Biblical Commentary' by Andrew T. Lincoln (Dallas, Word Books, 1990).

Other books
● In the course of the *Bible Guide* I refer to Dr Clinton E. Arnold's book *Ephesians: Power and Magic. The concept of power in Ephesians in light of its historical setting* (Cambridge, CUP, 1989), which gives much interesting background information.

● On the topic of 'spiritual warfare' I recommend Clinton Arnold's other book, *Powers of Darkness. A thoughtful, Biblical look at an urgent challenge facing the Church* (Leicester, IVP, 1992).

● On 'headship' and the relationship between men and women in marriage and in the Church I recommend Craig S. Keener, *Paul, Women & Wives: Marriage and Women's Ministry in the Letters of Paul* (Peabody, Hendrickson Publishers, 1992).

● Anyone interested in looking more closely at the 'critical' issues studied by the experts (e.g. Was it really by Paul? To whom was it written? And why? Does it copy Colossians? Is its message very different from the other letters of Paul?) can find a useful introduction to them all in Ernest Best, *Ephesians* (Sheffield, Sheffield Academic Press, 1993).